# Parenting
### at the
## Speed
### of Teens

# Parenting
## at the
# Speed
## of Teens

## *Positive Tips on Everyday Issues*

Foreword by Peter L. Benson, Ph.D.
*President, Search Institute*

Adapted from *When Parents Ask for Help:
Everyday Issues through an Asset-Building Lens*
(Copyright © 2003 Search Institute)
By Renie Howard

**Search** *Practical research
benefiting children
and youth*
INSTITUTE

*A Search Institute Publication*

## Parenting at the Speed of Teens: Positive Tips on Everyday Issues

Foreword by Peter L. Benson, Ph.D.

The contents of this book have been reviewed by a number of parenting and other professionals. Every effort has been made to provide sound advice; however, the information contained is not intended to take the place of appropriate counsel or other professional help in serious situations. The publisher and its reviewers take no responsibility for the use of any of the materials or methods described in this book, nor for the results thereof.

At the time of publication, all facts and figures cited herein are the most current available; all telephone numbers, addresses, and Web site URLs are accurate and active; all publications, organizations, Web sites, and other resources exist as described in this book; and all efforts have been made to verify them. The author and Search Institute make no warranty or guarantee concerning the information and materials given out by organizations or content found at Web sites that are cited herein, and we are not responsible for any changes that occur after this book's publication. If you find an error or believe that a resource listed herein is not as described, please contact Client Services at Search Institute.

10  9  8  7  6  5  4  3  2  1

Search Institute
615 First Avenue Northeast, Suite 125
Minneapolis, MN 55413
www.search-institute.org
612-376-8955 • 800-888-7828

**Credits**
Editor: Ruth Taswell
Book design and typesetting:
    Mary Ellen Buscher

**Library of Congress
Cataloging-in-Publication Data**
Parenting at the speed of teens : positive tips on everyday issues / foreword by Peter L. Benson.
    p. cm.
    Adaptation of: When parents ask for help : everyday issues through an asset-building lens : handouts for people raising adolescents / by Renie Howard.
    Includes bibliographical references.
    ISBN: 1-57482-845-2 (pbk. : alk. paper)
    1. Parent and teenager.  2. Teenagers—Family relationships.  3. Adolescence. I. Howard, Renie, 1955-  When parents ask for help.  II. Search Institute (Minneapolis, Minn.)
HQ799.15.P06  2004
649'.125–dc22

                                            2004004875

Printed in Canada on acid-free paper

**About Search Institute**
Search Institute is an independent, nonprofit, nonsectarian organization whose mission is to provide leadership, knowledge, and resources to promote healthy children, youth, and communities. The Institute collaborates with others to promote long-term organizational and cultural change that supports its mission. Search Institute's vision is a world where all young people are valued and thrive. For a free information packet, call 800-888-7828.

# Contents

# Foreword

What may seem to you as a parent to be routine—even inconsequential—is likely a lasting memory for your teen. What he or she remembers are often the little things—the back rubs, late-night conversations over cocoa, missed curfews (and resulting consequences), rituals of family mealtimes, help with homework, invitations to friends to "hang" around the kitchen or family room. Being an effective parent has more to do with everyday interactions than it does with the big stuff. The little ways you support, guide, inspire, encourage, and connect in the hubbub of life add up to make a big difference in the life of your teenager.

*Parenting at the Speed of Teens* is a practical, easy-to-use guide that offers positive, commonsense strategies for dealing with the ordinary issues of parenting teenagers: junk food, the Internet, stress, jobs, friends. And it shows how the basics of parenting can help with working through some of the more vexing issues (depression, divorce, racism, substance abuse) that sometimes surface. It illustrates how the daily conversations, boundaries, guidance, and modeling that you provide as a parent add up across many seemingly different issues and challenges.

This book is grounded in Search Institute's research on the everyday good stuff that young people need in their lives to help them grow up healthy, caring, and responsible. We call this good stuff, such as support, positive communication, and strong values, *developmental assets.* Research with 2 million teenagers consistently shows that having more of these assets in their lives makes a major difference in the choices teenagers make in life. We also sometimes call the assets *building blocks of healthy development* to emphasize the importance of piecing together many of these small building blocks across the years in creating a solid foundation for life.

As a parent, you play a vital role in building these assets, but you don't need to build assets alone. There are many adults in your extended family, your network of friends, and others who know your teenager; they can be great resources in the little (and sometimes big) ways they support, guide, and relate to your teenager. And don't forget that your maturing teenager also has a growing responsibility for her or his own development. Through the conversations and suggestions in this book, you'll find new ways to work together in your shared goal: your teenager growing up successfully.

Taking a positive, asset-building approach to parenting isn't glamorous or a "miracle cure." It doesn't take away all the irritations and frustrations that are inevitable in parenting. And it doesn't guarantee that nothing will go wrong. Sometimes things do, despite all your best efforts.

But building assets does increase the odds that your teenager will grow up well. It affirms the many ways you are already making a difference. It encourages you when you're wondering if anything is getting through. And it reminds you that the little stuff does, in the end, add up to make a big difference.

Peter L. Benson, Ph.D.
*President, Search Institute*

# INTRODUCTION
# Are You Enjoying the Ride?

Like a speeding roller coaster, raising teens can be a wild ride. Both joyous thrills and sheer terrors are likely to occur through the everyday ups and downs and the unexpected bumps and turns. But, as nerve-racking as the ride may sometimes be, it doesn't have to be a full-throttle vertical drop.

Adolescence is a time of rapid change, when a young person is busy figuring out who he or she is and wants to be. Seeing your teen become increasingly in-dependent while also contributing more to the family can be exciting and satisfying. At the same time, the role you have played for years as a parent may sud-denly be less clear, and you may not know what to do. Perhaps you're feeling frustrated, stressed out, maybe even at your wit's end.

It's tricky navigating the rapid changes and confu-sion a teenager goes through. But it's easier when you recognize that the issues that come up are due in part to underlying normal developmental changes, such as your teen's emerging sexual identity and a growing ability to think more independently. If you're used to helping your teen think things through, changes in behavior—such as responses limited to a single syllable or overdramatized annoyance and impatience with you—are naturally going to feel different and unsettling.

The reality is that it's normal for you to feel confused at times, just as it is for your teen. Episodes of "rebellion" are usually expressions of typical developmental change. Every teenager is an individual whose behavior must be interpreted in light of her or his uniqueness.

Every family also has its own set of circumstances and values; some behaviors are more acceptable in some families than others. Likewise, what may work with one individual teen or one family may not necessarily be ideal for another. For the usual sorts of teen issues, there aren't necessarily sure-fire prescriptive answers about what to say, when to say it, or how to say it that will work with every teen—there are simply too many variables.

So what can you do to make the roller-coaster ride more thrilling than terrifying in *your family?* What can you do to really make a difference in giving *your teen* what he or she needs to learn, grow, and flourish as an individual? This book can help.

## Igniting Positive Change

For your teen to grow up to be a caring, responsible, and happy adult, <u>you need to help her or him learn how to make wise choices, handle the pressures of daily living, and find meaning and fulfillment in life</u>. Making sure your teen has the resources—from within as well as from others—to cope with life's ups and downs makes it more likely that you won't have to ride through the adolescent years white-knuckled. The more positive resources your teens truly have, the more likely they will be able to hold on when life throws in some surprising twists and turns or to pick themselves up again after making a poor choice.

How much time do you spend thinking about what you *don't* want your teen to do or become? How much time do you spend thinking about how you *do* want your teen to grow up, what you want her or his life to look like—both now and in the future? Focusing on your teen's strengths and abilities can help you better identify the areas in which he or she has plenty of resources and those in which more support would be helpful.

## Steering Away from Obstacles

In the pages that follow, you'll find encouragement and hope along with sound, practical ideas that can work. This is not a whole treatise on parenting, nor is it intended to take the place of appropriate counseling or other professional help in serious situations with a troubled teen. Each chapter addresses an issue common to many adolescents, including curfews, dating, homework, grades, risky activities, conflicts, body image, depression, sibling fights, chores, jobs, and more.

Rather than viewing a specific issue merely as a problem, however, this book offers you a way to think differently. Each chapter provides a starting place for dealing with an adolescent issue through a positive lens. The practical tips can help you deal with each situation in upbeat, constructive ways that can help everyone involved feel better.

How do you start changing your thinking and priorities? That's where a positive approach comes in. You may be saying to yourself, "It's easy to have an optimistic approach to parenting young children, but teenagers?" Rest assured: despite the numerous negative images of adolescence, the vast majority of teens are looking for indications that adults—especially you—see the good inside them.

Taking a positive approach to parenting teens means focusing on their strengths and their normal developmental changes and needs rather than just on problems. When you adopt a positive perspective, it can alter many aspects of the way you interact with your teenager. For example, a common parenting perspective sees discipline mainly as *punishment;* with a positive perspective, you can view discipline mainly as a way to *teach* and *guide*.

In this book, the positive approach to raising an adolescent is grounded in the pioneering work of

Search Institute in Minneapolis, Minnesota, a nonprofit organization that conducts research on child and youth development. By focusing on developmental needs and exploring what children and youth really require to have successes in life, researchers at Search Institute identified 40 key "developmental assets" that have a tremendous influence on young people's lives. These assets—or positive experiences, opportunities, and qualities—help identify the vital resources young people require to pursue productive paths through life. (A complete list of the developmental assets appears at the back of this book on pages 108–110.)

The developmental assets encourage you not only to think about your teenager's life and particular strengths but also to examine your own life. The way you live your life has a powerful impact on how your teen internalizes the assets: What does the way you spend time and money say about what's important to you? How much time are you investing in doing things that nurture your teen's assets? For example, how much time do you spend trying to get her or him to clean up the bedroom versus affirming the specific ways he or she is helping out in the family or helping others?

The developmental assets give you concrete, practical ideas for focusing your thinking positively—to intentionally explore *how* to help your teen build upon the assets he or she has as well as to address areas where you and your teen see opportunities to grow. Taking an asset-building approach to your parenting

# Why Developmental Assets Are So Important

"Why do some kids grow up more easily, while others struggle?" This question and others like it have guided the research at Search Institute. The naming of the 40 developmental assets is just one of the institute's leading efforts to help make it easier to give kids what they truly need to succeed.

Search Institute researchers also designed a survey to measure the number of assets that students in grades 6 through 12 are experiencing in their lives. They found, in hundreds of different communities in the United States and Canada, that the more assets young people have, the more likely they are to make wise decisions, choose positive paths, manage the pressures inherent in life, be caring and responsible, and find meaning and fulfillment.

The assets represent everyday wisdom about experiences and characteristics that are important for young people. Hundreds of studies also support the significance of these assets. Research shows that the assets are powerful influences on adolescent behavior, both protecting young people from unhealthy behaviors and promoting positive attitudes and choices. This effect is evident across all cultural and socioeconomic groups of youth.

While the assets are powerful shapers of young people's lives and choices, too few experience many of these assets. Young people surveyed, on average, report having only about 19 assets.

Many factors influence why some young people have successes in life and why others have a harder time: economic circumstances, genetics, trauma, and more. But these factors aren't all that matters. Parents, other adults, and peers can influence the number of developmental assets a young person has.

Nurturing developmental assets in children and adolescents has tremendous potential for reducing many of the problems that concern parents and other adults. Intentionally focusing on increasing the number of assets a young person develops is known as "asset building." Everyone—not just parents and guardians, but also teachers, coaches, friends, neighbors, employers, and others—can help build a young person's assets.

means developing a relationship with your daughter or son that is positive and caring, spending valuable time together, and nurturing her or his strengths.

## Building Assets for and with Your Teen

Many of the things you do as a parent build your teen's *external assets*. These developmental assets are the relationships and opportunities that you and other adults, peers, and institutions provide.

The other 20 development assets are *internal*. These abilities, values, attitudes, and commitments are assets that your teen, with your help, can develop internally to help herself or himself now and later as an adult.

These external and internal assets are arranged in categories, each representing a key area of human development in a young person's life, such as "Support" or "Social Competencies." As parents, you can't dictate or force these characteristics to develop or expect that they will automatically occur. However, you can intentionally nourish and mold them.

Having assets doesn't make all the issues go away. After all, many issues come up because your teen is confronting normal developmental tasks of adolescence. The assets can, however, provide teens with the support and resources they need to overcome challenges they encounter. And the assets can provide you as a parent with help in choosing specific, incremental ways you want to build the strengths of your teen.

## How to Use This Book

To intentionally build your teen's developmental assets, you may want first to scan the table of contents to find the issue most pressing for you, or if you prefer, read the book from cover to cover for an overview. Beginning most chapters are a couple of statements or questions from parents about a common dilemma, followed by tips framed through an asset-building lens on how to deal with the issue—and build assets. To signify which of the eight development asset categories the tips support, the following icons are used:

**External Assets**

 Support

 Empowerment

 Boundaries and Expectations

 Constructive Use of Time

**Internal Assets**

 Commitment to Learning

 Positive Values

 Social Competencies

 Positive Identity

You also may want to try using the daily checklist (following the list of developmental assets on page 111), or create your own list if you wish to focus more deliberately on building on your teen's strengths rather than just solving problems.

## Nurture Your Own Assets

The asset-building approach focuses on children and adolescents, but parents need support, too. Just as asset building promotes teens and younger children being more connected to caring adults, it also encourages parents or guardians to strengthen their own connections within their communities. And because your teen's adolescence may be a challenging time in your life, it's particularly important to nurture your own strengths.

Making sure you get adequate support, taking time to take care of yourself, and allowing for your own personal growth as a parent and as an individual are consistent themes throughout this book. The more connected you are to sources of support—friends, family, neighbors, schools, faith-based organizations—the better prepared you will be to meet the challenges of parenting. Taking time for yourself, knowing when you need a break, and asking for help are important skills, not only for parenting, but also for being a healthy adult.

Parenting naturally changes your sense of who you are, but striving for growth in your own life is invaluable. Many of the issues discussed in this book ask you to examine your own attitudes and beliefs on a given topic so that you can more effectively help your teens explore who they are and their place in the world around them.

## Reaching Out

As a parent, you may often think that you have to take all the responsibility in parenting. In reality, other parents, extended family, neighbors, schools, and community agencies are potential asset-building partners. So is your teen.

As a maturing adolescent, your son or daughter

likely has good ideas about the kind of life he or she hopes to live and what's needed to make his or her own dreams come true. Teens have a lot to contribute to the family if you take seriously their perspectives and their unique gifts. Don't forget to ask *them* what they think! You can learn from your children, just as they do from you.

## Keep Loving Them

*Parenting at the Speed of Teens* is designed to help you meet parenting challenges with creativity and compassion—and to truly appreciate who your daughter or son is becoming. The more your teens recognize the importance of their own choices and the power they have to make those choices, the more likely they'll believe in their ability to do whatever they set out to do.

The assets are positive experiences and qualities that anyone can help bring into the lives of youth. But as a parent, you can start the engines running. Build on your own and on your teen's strengths, find sources of support, and, more than anything else, show her or him your love. You can do a lot to help make your teen's growing up be a more enjoyable ride—for both of you.

# Getting Along: Parents and Teens

*Your Dilemma:*

**"Sometimes I think Selena believes I was put here to be at her beck and call. I need her to understand how busy my schedule is, too."**
*or*
**"Every time Josh and I talk, he winds up yelling and slamming the door!"**

As the parent of a teen, you probably have days when you wish you could take a long break from parenting. The "job" sometimes just feels too hard. You may find yourself asking: Why is it so difficult to get along?

While you can't control your kid's behavior, you can control your own. You can do much to make life more peaceful in your home. By finding ways to show you're truly there for your teen, you can help create a home that feels supportive, positive, and loving for everyone.

### ☺ RESOLVE CONFLICTS PEACEFULLY

Let your teen know you expect disagreement at times, but you also expect everyone to work through conflict in agreed-upon ways. When conflicts arise, **really listen** to what your teen has to say, even if it doesn't seem to make sense. And **try not to interrupt or show impatience,** even if your teen does.

**Ask if you may give a suggestion**. If the answer is no, respect that. If it is "I don't care," go ahead and take the response as a yes and offer your idea. **If your discussion has become especially heated**, **take some time apart** before continuing.

### ♥ PROVIDE FAMILY SUPPORT

Show your love for your teen—without expecting anything in return. Say, "I love you"—don't assume he or she knows. **Be affectionate,** but respect your teen's "space." If a hug is too much, try a touch on the shoulder or write a special note.

**Spend time with each of your teens individually,** and make it clear that this time is valuable to you. It's important, too, to try to have at least **one family meal every day** and a special family night once a week, even if it seems that a night of fun rarely includes parents in your teen's mind. You *can* make a family night fun, and it doesn't have to be the *entire* evening. Let your teen choose the family activity.

### ♥ COMMUNICATE POSITIVELY AS A FAMILY

Let your teen know that you're always available to listen. **Try to hear what he or she is saying without judging, criticizing, or correcting.** Encourage your daughter or son to use words to describe emotions directly and constructively (e.g., "I feel really sad that Jessica's moving away" rather than "Why do we have to live in this stupid place?").

## Hints for Getting Along as a Family

Try using these hints as a discussion starter for your family. See which ones make sense. Feel free to rewrite them in words that work better for your family members.

| DO... | DO NOT... |
|---|---|
| Ask without yelling. | Whine. |
| Be willing to compromise. | Use the words *always* and *never* inaccurately. |
| Share willingly. | Tell each other's secrets. |
| Treat each other's property with care and respect. | Ignore each other's requests or snoop. |
| Take responsibility for your own actions and words. | Embarrass family members in front of their friends. |
| Be thoughtful of each other— especially if you know a family member's having a difficult day. | Make plans for another family member without checking with that person first. |

**Avoid making certain topics "off-limits."** You're entitled to some privacy, of course, and so is your teen. Make it clear that you'll do your best to answer sincere and respectful questions.

### VALUE YOUTH
**Ask your teen's opinions** on different matters. You may not agree with those opinions, but it's important to allow for safe discussion of ideas to show that you value your teen's input. Creating opportunities to share in responsibilities can be an important step toward a more mutual relationship, too.

### ⚅ SET FAMILY BOUNDARIES

**Set ground rules** for discussion in your family that everyone can uphold. Avoid ignoring each other's requests, telling each other's secrets, or embarrassing one another in front of friends. It helps to model healthy relationships with your own parents also.

### ⚅ KEEP EXPECTATIONS HIGH

**Be clear about what you expect** from your teen and *why* you have these expectations: because of her or his many talents, interests, and abilities! Ask whether your teen considers your expectations fair, and invite her or him to identify personal expectations. Remind your teen that high expectations are not just about obedience but also about reaching for a personal best and living up to potential. Also **ask your teen what expectations he or she has for you** as a parent.

### 👍 BUILD SELF-ESTEEM

When your teen makes mistakes, **distinguish between the behavior and who he or she is** (e.g., you might say, "I can see you're angry, but slamming the door is not acceptable" rather than, "Don't you dare slam that door again!"). Hold your teen accountable for actions, but **allow room to make mistakes** and realize limits.

### *SERVE YOUR KIDS WELL*

*Getting along with teens can be challenging at times, no doubt about it. Of course, they may feel the same way about getting along with adults. The skills you teach them—and model for them—for getting along with all family members will serve them well in everything they do.*

# Getting Along: Siblings

*Your Dilemma:*

**"Leticia keeps picking fights with Melissa because we spend a lot of time going to Melissa's gymnastics meets. I think she's jealous."**

*or*

**"Dan and Deanna are at it constantly. The fighting and yelling—it's driving me crazy."**

Living with brothers and sisters is most children's first experience in learning how to get along with other people. But no matter how well behaved your kids are, if there is more than one in the house, they will argue. Brothers and sisters are unique individuals who at times have conflicting or differing interests and needs, just as you and a spouse or partner may have. The question about sibling conflicts is, when should you

5

dive in—and how—and when should you let your kids work it out themselves?

### ♥ COMMUNICATE POSITIVELY AS A FAMILY

Reassure your teens that **disagreements are normal but constant fighting is upsetting,** and you value a peaceful home. It's important not to deny what one of your kids is feeling toward her or his sibling. **Teach them how to** use "I" statements to **express feelings directly without making accusations** (e.g., "I feel angry when you do that" instead of "You make me so mad" or "You are so stupid").

### ⭐ SET FAMILY BOUNDARIES

**Set firm limits about verbal exchanges.** For example, you might have a rule that name-calling isn't an acceptable way to express anger. Make it clear that some activities, such as play wrestling and tickling, are only allowed if both kids consider them fun.

If your kids choose to ignore your limits, remind them of consequences you previously determined together. Be consistent without shaming or blaming. Keep in mind that you may renegotiate boundaries to change over time—except for bottom-line issues of physical health and safety.

### ☺ RESOLVE CONFLICTS PEACEFULLY

The more you **stay out of normal bickering or minor fights,** the more likely it is that your teens will learn to settle differences on their own. **Get involved when the situation threatens to become emotionally or physically hurtful.** Acknowledge your kids' anger and give each a chance to speak. It's important not to take sides. Even though they are maturing in many ways, they still need your help in learning how to negotiate, compromise, share, and take turns. If they can't resolve the situation, give them time apart to think it over.

### ♥ PROVIDE FAMILY SUPPORT

**Avoid comparing one of your kids to another,** which can affect either's self-esteem and increase jealousy and envy. Encourage your teens to spend time together doing things they both enjoy. Teens don't always express their interests, or they may share only what they know you want to hear, so be sure to **affirm each of their unique talents even if they don't match yours or anyone else's in the family.**

### ☺ MODEL GOOD RELATIONSHIPS

**Let your children see you having good relationships with your own siblings.** Point out the qualities you like about your brothers or sisters. If you don't get along with your own siblings, talk about it. If your kids understand how hurting a brother's or sister's feelings can affect the relationship and everyone's self-esteem, they may be more careful about what they say and do with their siblings.

### *LOVE YOUR KIDS FOR WHO THEY ARE*

*Sibling fights happen for a variety of reasons—attention seeking, jealousy, competition, teasing. If you show your teens that you love each of them for who they are and help them learn how to communicate well and resolve conflict, you will give them what they need to enjoy other important relationships in their future.*

# TV

*Your Dilemma:*

**"Jamie just sits in front of the TV when he gets home from school. He barely says hello. He goes right for that remote."**

*or*

**"That show Renée watches is all about sex. Sure, the characters are teenagers. But they're all teenagers having sex!"**

Television can be fun and relaxing, and for many people, some TV programming also offers an educational and cultural connection to the outside world. But TV programming can also be violent, disturbing, stupid, or just plain loud. Often the center of many homes, a TV can fill up the "space" between family members, creating distance instead of connection.

When TV assumes too great a role in your teen's life (or in yours), its hypnotic effects can drain time

8

and energy for other activities. Fortunately, you can put TV in its place and point out various reasons and alternatives for moving off the couch.

### ⭐ SET FAMILY BOUNDARIES

To avoid continuous fighting, **talk with your teen about what's okay to watch and how often**—while the TV set is turned off. Talk about the values communicated in TV shows and how they relate to your family's own values. Work together to set clear boundaries and explain why certain boundaries are important (e.g., it's okay to watch educational shows but not daytime talk shows).

**Put the TV in a less prominent location**—not the living room or your teen's bedroom—so that it's not the focal point of your home life. When TV watching is less frequent and its presence less obvious, and your teens are reading more, playing games and music, or involved in other activities, they may end up losing some interest in it.

### ⭐ BE A ROLE MODEL

Think about your own viewing habits. **Are there changes you could make** that would affect how *you* live? The choices you make about watching TV send messages to the rest of the family.

### 💡 READ FOR PLEASURE

**Encourage your teen to read anything that appeals to her or him**—books, poetry, magazines, picture books, even comic books. Keep in mind that some teens may prefer nonfiction. Give them books you loved when you were their age. Offer a magazine subscription as a holiday or birthday gift.

**Let your teen see you enjoying reading.** Read aloud to each other pieces that make you laugh or touch you in some way. Encourage your son or daughter to read to younger siblings or to older adults at senior residences.

**For a hard-to-convince teen,** rent videos of books and drop hints of how the book had lots more details. For a reluctant reader, leave books around to discover—you may even leave notes inside them about your favorite parts.

### What If My Kid Says, "I'm Bored"?

Don't despair—let the boredom set in. Turning off the TV can be hard, especially if your teen rolls her or his eyes at any alternatives you suggest. If life has been particularly busy lately, and you haven't had enough time to encourage your teen to try some new activities, turning off the TV can feel equally disheartening.

But teens will find a way out of the boredom eventually—staring into space, daydreaming, calling friends, planning what to wear, journaling, reading magazines, doing sit-ups, and more. *Parents don't always have to figure out how to fill in the gaps.*

### BE CREATIVE

**Promote artistic interests,** such as music, drawing, acting, and writing. Such activities can help teens achieve in other subjects (e.g., drawing helps writing, drama makes history vivid) and give them positive, healthy ways to express conflicting emotions and get a handle on the ups and downs of the teen years.

Display your teen's work or encourage him or her to perform for others. (Parents often do this for younger children but stop as children get older.) Avoid putting anyone on the spot. **Plan ahead to schedule time as a family** to listen to music, go to a museum (most have a free day), attend a play (school per-

formances are free or inexpensive), or watch a video performance or concert.

### ⊕ ENCOURAGE YOUTH PROGRAMS
Help your teen **find structured activities that appeal to
individual interests,** particularly during after-school hours
when he or she might otherwise be home alone. Getting involved in clubs, recreational or athletic activities, or cultural or
faith-based youth groups can help teens feel more connected
with other people their age. These are opportunities to actively
do something they enjoy rather than just passively watch
others.

## *NURTURE CONNECTIONS*
*The more you can help your teen find meaningful connec-
tions in daily life—with other people, with nature, with
books and sports, music and art—the less likely he or she is
to feel disconnected and to rely on an inactive form of entertainment. By turning off the TV more often than turning it
on, you can provide the quiet your child needs to hear life
calling.*

# The Internet

*Your Dilemma:*

**"It seems like Sydney's on the computer 24/7. She never gets outside or reads a book anymore."**
*or*
**"I'm worried about Julio. I think he may have 'met' someone older online."**

How do you monitor your teen's time on the Internet without making her or him feel you're interfering too much? Web filters and online services are one way to help protect children from the Internet's negative influences. But they're certainly no cure-all, and sometimes they actually block young people from good content designed especially for them.

The Internet is an amazing portal to learning and exploring opportunities, but like TV and video games, it can suck away time in an inactive way. When dealing with Internet issues, you can help keep your kid safe from the array of potential threats and pitfalls without overriding its usefulness and fun.

### ⬟ SET FAMILY BOUNDARIES

**Agree on limits to Internet use** that seem as fair as possible to both you and your teen. Be prepared to make adjustments. To help balance time playing Internet-based games and instant messaging friends, encourage your daughter or son to seek out sites that relate to suitable hobbies and interests. **Consider keeping the computer located where it is easier to informally monitor your teen's Internet use** (e.g., in the kitchen, not in your teen's bedroom) and to reduce isolated time spent on the computer.

### ♥ COMMUNICATE POSITIVELY AS A FAMILY

**Ask your teen about favorite Web sites and why he or she likes them.** Emphasize what you hope your teen will get out of surfing. Spend time surfing the net together. Let your daughter teach you some of what she knows, or ask your son to do some information gathering for the family (e.g., for a trip).

Make sure your teen knows that you're using filters for protection from others, not because you do not trust her or him to use the Internet responsibly. **If your teen comes across any uncomfortable information** (e.g., pornographic sites), encourage discussions about it. Let your child know you realize it may feel embarrassing, but reassure her or him of your support. **Be sure to talk about safety tips (see next page).**

### ✹ ENSURE SAFETY

If your teen is shy, the Internet may be especially appealing because it's often easier to talk to people online than in person. But you should **instruct your son or daughter never to give out personal information.** Most often this information is used for advertising purposes, but from time to time, unsafe adults use it to coerce or harm young people.

## An Internet Safety Checklist

Let your teen know that her or his safety is important to you. Ask your daughter or son to follow these safety tips,* and consider posting them on the computer monitor or desk so that they can be easily seen:

- ◆ Don't give out your address, phone number, and name and location of your school or other personal information. Remember that not everyone may be who they say they are.
- ◆ Keep your passwords secret, even from friends.
- ◆ Use a nickname in chat rooms, so that you can exit if someone makes you uncomfortable, and your screen name won't make it easy to trace you.
- ◆ Never send anyone your photo (without checking with a parent or guardian first).
- ◆ Never agree to get together in person with anyone you "meet" online (without making sure it's okay with your parent or guardian. If they say it's okay, only meet in a public place and bring your parent or guardian along).
- ◆ Never respond to any mean or hurtful messages and never write any threats, which is breaking the law.

*Adapted from the National Center for Missing and Exploited Children at the Web site accessed February 13, 2004: www.missingkids.com.

### BE HONEST
Because people often misrepresent themselves and information is often misleading on the Internet, **teach your teen to question what is shown online—that it's not all necessarily**

**believable.** Talk with your son or daughter, too, about being honest and avoiding the temptation to misrepresent who he or she is.

## ☺ PROMOTE CULTURAL COMPETENCE
**Encourage your teen to correspond with young people from different countries.** Many pen pal sites on the Web (check with the language teachers at your teen's school or a librarian for a current safe reference) will connect young people who have similar interests. With an easy way to exchange information about what teen life is like in different places, your son or daughter can learn about different cultures as well as gain a deeper understanding of his or her own cultural identity.

## *GET AND GIVE GUIDANCE*
*When used with care, the Internet can be fun, safe, and an excellent source of information and means of communication. Don't hesitate to find out what the Internet policy is at your local library and at your teen's school and adopt a similar guideline for your family. Ask librarians and teachers, as well as other Internet users, for additional tips and guidance so that your teen can make the most of the Internet.*

# Chores

*Your Dilemma:*

**"His room is a disaster.
All I ask is to see the carpet again."**

*or*

**"Sheila's got homework and softball practice
keeping her busy during the week.
Is it too much to ask for help with
dinner on Sunday night?"**

*Chores.* Few people enjoy doing them, but they are an inevitable part of life. To gain the confidence necessary to eventually live independently, teens need to learn how to handle chores among their other responsibilities. Teaching them to handle chores helps them develop valuable planning and scheduling skills. And they can learn a variety of life lessons from doing chores, such as the importance of cooperation, self-discipline, and self-reliance. So how do we help our children learn to embrace this necessary aspect of daily life?

### ⯃ SET FAMILY BOUNDARIES

Create an understanding with your teen that chores are an expected part of family life. Tell them that teens are "adults in training." To teach some life skills and include your teen in the decision making, you may want to **ask that everyone rotate doing different chores each week, rather than just making assignments.**

**It is important to encourage sons and daughters to share the same tasks** and not do certain duties because of their gender. Both girls and boys need to know how to do a variety of jobs from basic repairs and yard work to cooking and laundry.

**The first couple of times your teen does a task, do it together.** That way, you can show how to do it and set standards for each chore—don't assume your daughter or son will know. Avoid giving your teen a long list to remember—a written checklist is helpful.

### ⯃ VALUE YOUTH

**Doing chores emphasizes that teens have useful roles within the family.** Here are just some of the age-appropriate ways they can be helpful:

- ◆ Meal preparation: budgeting and shopping for meals, cooking, setting and clearing the table, serving, cleaning up;
- ◆ Cleaning: of their own room, of family areas (e.g., bathroom and kitchen), straightening up, dusting, and vacuuming;
- ◆ Laundry: sorting by color, washing and drying, folding, putting away;

- ◆ Maintenance: yard work, painting, simple repairs, car maintenance;
- ◆ Child care: help with younger brothers and sisters;
- ◆ Pet care; and
- ◆ Recycling, collecting, and taking out the garbage.

## ♥ PROVIDE FAMILY SUPPORT

Doing big chores as a group, such as cleaning out the garage, can be a way to bring the family together. You might make regular chores a weekly event and do those together, too. Encourage everyone to be thoughtful: *If the trash can is full, empty it. If you use the last of the toilet paper, get out a fresh roll.* **Always compliment your teen for doing a good job or point out when he or she is being helpful.** It's gratifying to feel appreciated, and positive feedback is encouraging.

## TAKE PERSONAL RESPONSIBILITY

Show your teen a good example: **follow through on your own chores** and what you say you'll do. It is difficult for a teen to understand why a parent can have a messy bedroom, while insisting that it's not okay for the teen's room to be messy.

## *A JOB WELL DONE*

*When you teach your teen responsibility through chores, he or she learns to become an integral part of a smooth-running household. This will be invaluable and much appreciated when your teen moves out of your home and manages chores on her or his own.*

# Curfew

*Your Dilemma:*

**"Mom, I'm going out with Darnel and the guys. I'll be home later. Maybe around midnight, I'm not sure. See you, bye."**
*or*
**"Tanya just turned 15. She wants to start staying out until midnight on Saturdays. I don't know what to do."**

In most teens' minds, there probably couldn't be any better way to assert their independence than to stay out late, hanging out with friends away from home. And if your teen has previously tended to be less social, this might actually be a welcome step in her or his increasing maturity. But teens are not yet adults and still need protection and guidance. By including your teen in decisions about routine curfews and coming to a reasonable compromise, you can make curfew less of a hot-button topic.

## ENSURE SAFETY

Before they head out the door, it is important to **find out where teens are going** (and a telephone number where they can be reached), **who will be with them, how they're getting there and back, and when they plan to be home.** If your teen is going to be walking around with friends or changing location, request telephone updates so that you know he or she is okay.

Some young people appreciate having **a curfew since it gives them a good excuse for getting out of uncomfortable situations.** Reassure your teen, too, that if trouble arises, he or she can always call you or another trusted adult.

## COMMUNICATE POSITIVELY AS A FAMILY

**Say how much you appreciate it when your teen tells you where he or she is going to be and comes home on time.** Often, the more information teens provide to parents, the more freedom parents are likely to provide to the kids.

State directly to your teen the dangers that concern you. Ask what curfew he or she thinks is fair. If your teen questions why some of his or her friends get to stay out later, explain why you see the need for that difference. **Review and adjust curfews together regularly** as your child gets older, more mature, or shows increased responsibility.

## SET FAMILY BOUNDARIES

**Make sure your teen is aware of your expectations and knows there will be consequences for ignoring curfew,** such as a more restrictive curfew the next time. You may want to allow a 5- or 10-minute grace period, or request a phone call if your son or daughter can't be home on time. **Be consistent in enforcing consequences.**

### ⬟ BE A ROLE MODEL
**When *you* go out, be equally considerate:** communicate where you're going and when you plan to be home, and call if *you'll* be late.

## *TIME IS ON YOUR SIDE*

*Without a curfew to guide and protect teens, they very well may stay up all night and sleep all day, missing out on school and daily life. By including your daughter or son in negotiating what are fair expectations and consequences, you can maintain some safe boundaries while still allowing some of the necessary independence at this time in her or his life.*

# Junk Food

*Your Dilemma:*

**"As soon as he gets home from school, Jesse goes right for the chips and cookies. I think he's allergic to healthy food."**

*or*

**"I wish Theresa would eat something other than soda and fries for lunch every day."**

A craving for junk food seems to go hand in hand with the teenage years. Chips, pizza, sweets, and fast food are often the major food groups. With teens having more authority over food choices than they did when they were younger, it's also another way for them to assert their independence. If the family eats meat, they may become vegetarian. Or if the family is vegetarian, they may start eating meat.

Getting your teen to eat a decent meal regularly can be challenging. Add on your family's busy schedule, and you've got a recipe for nutritional breakdown. You can help slow your teen down long enough to get regular good meals by making a special commitment beyond just keeping the kitchen stocked with fresh fruit and vegetables.

### ♥ COMMUNICATE POSITIVELY AS A FAMILY

To help your teen appreciate the reality of "you are what you eat," **discuss connections between food choices and how a person feels and performs.** Encourage your son or daughter to notice how different foods can cause sluggishness or provide good energy. If your teen does decide to become a vegetarian, help research recipes and plan meals together to ensure he or she can make informed choices and get the necessary proteins and nutrients.

### ♥ PROVIDE FAMILY SUPPORT

Talking with your teen about the importance of sharing meals as a family is a key ingredient in creating a healthier diet for everyone. Taking time to sit together and share a meal gives you and your teen a chance to spend time with the people you love, to remember what you appreciate about each other, and to be grateful for all you have. **Try to have at least one meal together every day.**

### ☀ VALUE YOUTH

**When teens have the opportunity to learn how to cook**—whether from a parent or through a class—**they gain a practical skill that will serve them well when they're out on their own.** Let your teen do the cooking one night a week (or month), or prepare a meal to freeze and eat later. You may occasionally consider setting a reasonable budget, and having your son or daughter plan the menu and do the shopping be-fore preparing the meal.

### PROMOTE CULTURAL COMPETENCE
**Help your teen understand food's important connec-tion to your own cultural background.** Use time around the table and culturally related food to tell stories about your fam-ily. Explore new kinds of foods together: visit a farmers' market or grocery store that caters to an ethnic group that's different from yours.

### SERVE OTHERS
Encourage your teen or the whole family to **volunteer for a hunger-relief organization.** Serving meals to homeless families or raising money to end hunger gives kids a chance to contribute meaningfully to the community and to appreciate the food they have. Invite your teen to make the choices for your family's contribution.

### HOME COOKING
*If teens appreciate what goes into a nutritious meal and what it takes to prepare such a meal—and share in the re-sponsibility—they'll be nourishing more than just their phys-ical well-being. The world of food can be a great teaching tool for learning about a wide variety of topics—from menu planning and meal preparation to budgeting and cultural diversity.*

# School and Homework

*Your Dilemma:*

**"Camryn seems bored with school.
She doesn't even bring books home to study."**
*or*
**"Pete is overloaded with homework.
He can barely keep up."**

Even if you didn't particularly enjoy your school years or didn't complete your schooling, you have a lot to teach your child and you can show how learning can be exciting and fun. No matter how teens feel about school and homework, the fact remains that without at least a high school education, it will be very difficult for them to have the life they want.

### ⭐ KEEP EXPECTATIONS HIGH

When you expect the best from your teen, you're showing that you believe in her or him. Look for ways to acknowledge your teen's personal potential. **Avoid negative global comments about who he or she is,** such as, "What's the matter with you?" which can hurt self-esteem. Reassure your teen that mistakes and setbacks happen and be encouraging about expectations for the future.

## ♥ GET INVOLVED IN SCHOOLING

A high predictor of student success is parent involvement in schooling. **Let your teen see that you care about her or his school.** Speak with your teen's teachers, post the school calendar prominently at home, and attend school events as a family.

**If your teen is struggling, bored, or unhappy at school,** try to find out calmly what's at the root of the problem: "Are the classes too hard or easy? Do you feel safe at school? Are you feeling sad or depressed?" If your teen responds better to less direct probing, ask open-ended questions, such as, "What challenges you at school?" or "What can I do to help you succeed at school?" Find out what additional resources are available (e.g., peer or adult tutoring, a different teacher or even school, a guidance counselor or skilled therapist, or testing for a learning disability).

## ☼ MAKE THE MOST OF HOMEWORK

Doing at least one hour of homework every school day is one of the developmental assets that helps adolescents stay on track. **Encourage your teen to think, "I can do this."**

**Also help your teen find out how he or she learns best** (audio, visual, hands on, etc.) to make the most of study time. For the tips and ideas below, keep in mind that what works best for one person may differ for others:

◆ Provide a place to study that suits what your teen needs

to concentrate. Does he or she prefer a setting free of distractions (e.g., TV noise or people talking on the phone), some soft noise or minimal activity (e.g., radio playing or a coffee shop), or no noise (e.g., library)?

◆ Establish a regularly scheduled time for doing homework. Should it be before any TV watching or Internet surfing (right after school or a school activity)? Or would relaxing for a while with something to eat and drink be more beneficial?

◆ Suggest that your teen start with what he or she can manage best, whether that means the most difficult or the easiest assignment. Help create a sense of accomplishment that encourages more effort and achievement.

◆ Praise your teen for completing and handing in her or his homework.

## ACKNOWLEDGE SCHOOL ACHIEVEMENT

When your teen does well or improves in a class or on a test, **be sure to connect the achievement with keeping up with homework assignments.** If your son or daughter is struggling with unsatisfactory grades, work together on a homework plan that might yield better results in the future. When you frequently show how proud you are of good grades, you give the student incentive for ongoing success.

## CARE ABOUT SCHOOL

School spirit is a great asset for teens. **Help yours find a supervised club, sport, or other school activity to connect with school.** Find out and talk to them about famous or successful school alums. If your teens feel they belong at school, they'll be more invested in what goes on there and more likely to contribute positively to their school.

## 💡 COMMIT TO LEARNING

**When you share your own excitement about the world, you help your teens want to learn.** Teach them how to do something that you enjoy, or tell them about a class you're taking or an event you attended—even take a class together! If possible, show them your school pictures or report cards, or tell a story about a favorite teacher. Talk about what challenged you academically and socially and how you dealt with it.

## *THE MEANING OF SCHOOL*

*When teens see how schoolwork fits into their dreams for the future, they'll more likely follow through on what they know they have to do. At the same time, they'll gain a stronger sense of their own ability to do what they want successfully. You can support your teen's efforts by showing that you care very much about what he or she is getting out of school.*

# Graduation and Beyond

*Your Dilemma:*

**"Rochelle has such a hard time making the connection that what she does today will affect her future."**

*or*

**"Wes doesn't seem to have any goals. Yesterday he said that he doesn't intend to go to college."**

The high school years are a unique borderland between childhood and adulthood. Your teen probably amazes you sometimes with wisdom and maturity, and at other times, surprises you with less-than-mature judgment and defiance.

Your teen may move away from home just after or within a few years of high school graduation, a move that you may experience with a mix of joy and sorrow. Navigating this transition requires special attention to your needs as well as those of your son or daughter.

What can you do to make sure you feel excited about your own life as you prepare to let your teen go? Strengthening the family's bonds now will help make the transition easier when it comes and will give your son or daughter a profound sense of the love and acceptance of home.

## ☺ PLAN AHEAD AND MAKE THOUGHTFUL DECISIONS

**It may take some time before your teen connects what he or she does today with what he or she can do tomorrow.** Most adolescents eventually make the developmental leap, though some may have narrowed options with poor grades, or may have to do some catch-up work to pursue their dreams.

**Teens need coaching to learn the process of making careful decisions.** Adults can encourage them to gather information first and help them explore potential consequences. You might ask your teen questions to illustrate the issue from various points of view. For example, does he or she really *need* a car, or just *want* one? What sacrifices might be necessary in order to make it happen? Does he or she earn enough at a part-time job?

## ♥ COMMUNICATE POSITIVELY AS A FAMILY

**Start talking *now* about what your teen plans to do after high school.** Encourage each one to create a plan that suits her or his goals and ambitions, whether more education or a job is a part of the picture. Share your thoughts and expectations, but **be careful not to impose your own interests and goals.**

## FIND A SENSE OF PURPOSE

**Share your feelings about what is meaningful in your own life.** Ask your teen what he or she hopes to accomplish in life. **Discuss the values you think are important to carry.** Ask if your son or daughter agrees with those values and how to express those values in life—by seeking education, carefully choosing jobs, or setting goals.

## SEEK ROLE MODELS

If your teen is unsure about what he or she wants, **help find someone to discuss what a particular job is really like.** Questions to ask may include: "What's involved in your work?" "How did you get into it?" and "Do you enjoy what you do?"

## PROMOTE A POSITIVE FUTURE

**Look forward to the future with hope and enthusiasm and convey this optimism to your teen.** It's okay to talk about concerns regarding the future, but avoid making negative predictions—either in a personal or a global realm (e.g., it's better to say, "If you want to get a better grade, it might help to study more" rather than, "You'll never do well if you don't study more").

**Affirm your teen's dreams, even if they're not what you had in mind.** Support your son or daughter's pursuit of them as much as you sincerely can. If dreams are unrealistic (e.g., wanting to attend an Ivy League college when grades are low) or dangerous (e.g., to be a race car driver), teens might benefit from thinking through the real-life situations they want to experience, what they might need to learn, what strengths they already have to help them, and what else they'll need to get there.

### TAKE PERSONAL RESPONSIBILITY

**Help your teen learn to manage money responsibly** and to plan and save to attain goals. Talk about the importance of creating a budget and setting aside money (for fun, savings, and worthy causes), and show your daughter or son how to balance a checkbook. **Use logical consequences for irresponsible behavior** (e.g., hold your teen accountable for overuse charges on a cell phone).

## *PREPARE FOR THE LAUNCH*

*Even when teens become adults out on their own, parents can continue to guide them throughout their lives—if they're open to that. The love and acceptance they experience now will help prepare them for decisions about the future.*

# Bullying/Being Bullied

*Your Dilemma:*

**"Mike doesn't want to go to school. He says he feels ill all the time. I'm worried that something's going on."**
*or*
**"I just got a call from an upset parent. Kendra told some really nasty lies about another girl at school."**

Anyone can be a bully. Some may tend to be more physical, pushing and hitting. Others tend to use quieter behavior, such as spreading lies or deliberately excluding others. If your teen is being bullied, take seriously how truly anguishing this can be for a young person. Recognize that even persistent teasing by friends, siblings, or parents can cause stinging loneliness. Some teens find the pain so unbearable, they attempt suicide.

## ❤ COMMUNICATE POSITIVELY AS A FAMILY

**Don't let a bullying matter become a painful secret for your teen.** Make sure he or she knows to come to you if someone is being intimidating. Anytime your teen confides a fear or worry, tell her or him, "I'm really glad you told me that." Avoid teasing about any fears—it's a sure way to discourage talking. **Acknowledge how difficult and frightening the situation must be.** Assure your teen that you will do everything you can to ensure her or his safety, then follow through.

If you suspect something is going on, but your teen isn't talking about it, ask questions: "Do you feel safe in the school hallways?" or "Is there trouble on the bus?" Watch for clues, such as increased anxiety or not wanting to go to school. **Make it clear that being bullied is not her or his fault, and that it is wrong.**

## ☺ TEACH RESISTANCE SKILLS

**Teach your teen some basic resistance and conflict resolution skills that can help deflect the bullying.** Encourage her or him to try to walk away, sit near the driver on the bus, stay in areas where there are other students and teachers, and avoid being in the bathroom or locker room alone. Suggest that your teen "act as if the bullying does not bother you." **Those who bully will often stop if they don't get the response they're looking for.**

## ☀ ENSURE SAFETY

If bullying continues or includes repeated threats or physical harm, report it to the school immediately. Even if your teen is adamant about not contacting the school for fear of being labeled a "snitch," **let her or him know that trying to**

**handle it alone is not always appropriate.** Most schools are required to have a policy on dealing with bullying and should take action—especially when the specific behavior is also against the law.

### CREATE A SAFE, CARING SCHOOL

If you feel that no one at the school is helping your teen, talk to the principal about how the school policy on bullying applies to your teen's situation. **If there is no policy, talk with other parents, teachers, and the principal about creating one.**

### CARE ABOUT OTHERS

**When teens see others being bullied, assure them that they *can* help put a stop to it**—by taking a stand against bullying. Make it clear that you expect your daughter or son to refuse to join in if someone is teasing another person. Suggest that he or she report any bullying to a teacher or other trusted adult.

### TAKE PERSONAL RESPONSIBILITY

**If your teen is doing the bullying, seek help immediately.** Bullying is a sign of emotional distress and can lead to serious problems. Show that you love your teen but do not approve of her or his behavior.

**It's important that your teen take responsibility for bullying actions and the consequences.** Help her or him to understand the behavior by asking: "What did you do?" "Whom did you hurt?" "What were you trying to accomplish?" and "Do you think that was a positive goal?" Support school staff in the disciplinary action taken. Try to patiently help your teen sort through making an apology.

## FEEL SAFE AT SCHOOL

*To see your teen fear getting out of bed in the morning to go to school, or to learn that your teen may be hurting others, is heartbreaking. But if you take bullying seriously, you can help your son or daughter develop the support and skills to deal effectively with conflict and live in the world with confidence and assurance.*

# Violence at School

*Your Dilemma:*

**"Raj said a student hit a teacher
with a chair at school today."**
*or*
**"Antoine came home very upset. He overheard
two students threatening to hurt another kid."**

Fears about safety at school may be very real for
teens, affecting their schoolwork and physical well-
being. Some students may skip school to avoid what
frightens them, or bring their own weapons to school
for protection. Seeing that teachers are affected, too—
by focusing more on disciplining disruptive behavior
than on helping students learn—can also be distress-
ing. The causes of school violence vary: peer pressure,
gangs, cliques, alienation, crowding, truancy, easy ac-
cess to guns, the effects of alcohol and other drugs,
and violence in the media or in the home can all con-

tribute to the problem. Even if your teen has not experienced violence at school, it's important to help her or him recognize warning signs in other people's behavior and identify the safety precautions to take.

## ♥ ENCOURAGE RELATIONSHIPS WITH OTHER ADULTS

One of the most important means of heading off violence at school is ensuring that young people feel they have caring adults to confide in. **If your teen is threatened or has heard of a threat, encourage her or him to report it immediately to a trusted adult, or to school officials and law enforcement.** In the United States, students may also call the nationwide Speak Up Campaign hotline at 866-773-2587 to anonymously report weapon-related threats at schools. **Let your teen know that being honest and open is a responsibility when it comes to preventing possible violence at school.**

## ENSURE SAFETY

**If you keep guns in your home, speak to your teens about proper uses of guns** (e.g., not to solve arguments or get back at people who've hurt your feelings) **and take safety precautions.** Lock up all firearms and keep the key hidden. Use trigger guards on each weapon, and lock up ammunition separately from firearms.

## CARE ABOUT SCHOOL

Recent research suggests that school shootings are related mostly to young people feeling disconnected from their schools. **Encourage your teen to take an active role at school.** Suggest that your son or daughter join or start a peer mediation group, hold a peace rally, ask the school newspaper to

# Spotting the Warning Signs

Using the list below, talk with your teen about the potential warning signs of violent behavior. Explain that if a person behaves in the following ways, it doesn't mean he or she will automatically hurt another person—these are just some factors that have been recognized in people who have committed violent acts.

◆ Plays with weapons of any kind.

◆ Brags about acts of violence he or she would like to commit.

◆ Repeatedly watches violent programs or plays violent video games.

◆ Bullies or threatens other people.

◆ Acts cruelly to pets or other animals.

◆ Talks to others about being bullied and feels isolated, angry, depressed, and frustrated by the situation.

◆ Destroys property out of anger. Has been truant, suspended, or expelled from school.

◆ Has few or no close friends.

◆ Has had lots of disciplinary problems at school or run-ins with the police.

◆ Steals others' belongings or destroys property.

◆ Makes racist comments.

◆ Acts rudely to other people.

◆ Deals drugs or appears to belong to a gang.

If your son or daughter, or someone he or she knows, shows a number of these warning signs, seek help immediately. Tell a guidance counselor or school official. If necessary, call the police.

write stories on violence prevention, or set up an anonymous hotline where students can share concerns.

## 🕐 USE TIME CONSTRUCTIVELY

**Encourage your teens to get involved in other activities besides watching TV or playing video games, which often skew perceptions of violence.** The American Academy of Pediatrics suggests that parents limit the amount of TV kids watch to one to two hours per day. Encourage your teens to try music, theater, art classes, sports, clubs, community organizations, or congregational activities.

## *MAKE SCHOOL LEARNING SAFE*

*Pay attention to what your teen needs and keep the lines of communication open—with her or his friends as well. Make sure they all know they can come to you when they need to, and that they'll always have a safe place with you.*

# Friends

*Your Dilemma:*

**"DeShawn is hanging out with a new crowd we're not so sure we can trust. He's come home late a few nights and doesn't always tell us where he's going."**

*or*

**"Danielle just got in a huge fight with her friend, Nancy. We like Nancy and would like them to work things out."**

As teens become more independent, parents may feel pushed out of their lives and may not necessarily like all their friends. No matter how the situation may appear, your teen really does want you in his or her life. Offering your guidance and support to help your son or daughter find the way through the swirling social waters requires both generosity and restraint.

♥ **PROVIDE FAMILY SUPPORT**

**Get to know your teen's friends.** Be home when they're over and try to have at least a three- to five-minute conversation with them. Respect their privacy, but make the effort to find out what's going on in their lives. Let them know you're genuinely glad they're there and make your home a place where they feel welcome to hang out. **Get to know their parents or guardians, too.**

☺ **MODEL GOOD RELATIONSHIPS**

Know that **it is natural for some teens to have one or two close friends** rather than many friends, **but sometimes having few friends is a sign of not having enough friendship skills.** Help your teen learn about interacting with others in informal settings by showing how to make small talk or encouraging your son or daughter to ask others questions. Introduce your teen to people of many different ages. **When greeting other adults, be sure to acknowledge teens and their friends by introducing them.**

☺ **RESOLVE CONFLICTS PEACEFULLY**

As much as it may ache for you to hear your daughter or son voice the belief that "Everyone hates me," **avoid trying to "fix" the inconsistency of your teen's friendships.** Supply the moral support that will help your teen get through the hard times and learn how to manage the disappointment.

**You can help your son or daughter** *think* **through a situation, rather than just** *feel* **the way through it.** For example, ask leading questions regarding what the other person intended. When a relationship sours or fades, let your teen grieve, and let her or him know you're available to listen.

## Talking about Friends

The following questions may be helpful in starting a discussion with your teen about friends. Be sure to listen carefully and without judgment to what your daughter or son has to say.

◆ What do you and your friends have in common? What don't you have in common?

◆ What do you value in your friends? What do they value in you?

◆ Is it easy for you to make and keep friends? If not, what seems to cause problems?

◆ What is difficult or easy in having a friendship with a person of a different gender? Do you find it easier or more challenging to have a friendship with a person of the same gender?

◆ How balanced are your friendships? Do you tend to give or take more?

◆ Who can you count on?

◆ If you have ever felt rejected by a friend, how did you handle the rejection? Do you still think about it?

◆ What have you learned through your friendships?

## ⭐ ENCOURAGE POSITIVE FRIENDSHIPS

Keep remarks about your teen's friends upbeat. Affirm the friendships you regard as positive, but also **make an effort to reach out to the friends you find less appealing. Your own biases may have kept you from seeing their positive traits.**

If you're concerned that a situation is getting out of hand with a particular friend or group of friends, express your concerns calmly, and listen closely to what your teen has to say.

Try to find some grounds for agreement. For example, you might say, "Arthur is welcome here anytime, but I don't want you driving with him." **Young people often welcome limits, even if they don't admit it.**

Sometimes kids get involved with a worrisome group of friends because they're looking for a place to belong or to fit in. Help your teen look at her or his own strengths and choose healthy ways to connect with others.

### ⭐ BE A ROLE MODEL
**Call on your own friends.** Not only can they support you through the challenges of raising teens, but they can also help you model the high value you place on friendship, the time and energy you invest in staying connected, how you work through disappointments with them, or set boundaries on relationships that are draining.

### *SURROUNDED BY FRIENDS*
*Much about friendships teens simply have to work out for themselves. You can help by offering your support and acknowledging your son's or daughter's woes. With your guidance from the sidelines, your teen will learn how to be a good friend and to have good friends.*

# Other Caring, Responsible Adults

*Your Dilemma:*

**"Sometimes I feel overwhelmed and as if my wife and I are not enough. I wish there were some other adults Kai could spend time with."**

*or*

**"Could Julie possibly have any role models in her life besides singers and actresses?"**

If you live far from extended family or longtime friends, managing the ups and downs of the teen years may be especially trying. Imagine what a relief you might feel if your teen could regularly turn for support and encouragement to other trusted adults besides you. Think how much better off your teen's life might be as well. You would be no less important in his or her life—together, you would simply have the support of others who care.

Even without extended family nearby, you don't

have to do everything yourself. You can help your son or daughter establish several friendships with other caring adults. In doing so, you can be sure that your teen's life—and your own—will be that much richer.

### ♥ PROVIDE FAMILY SUPPORT

Teens will often listen to good advice from a nonparent that would just make them angry hearing it from a parent. **Ask your teen about a caring adult he or she might be interested in getting to know better.** Make a list together of the adults your teen has regular contact with, such as teachers, coaches, neighbors, bus drivers, and employers. **See if there are *trusted* adults who might be available** to spend time with your teen occasionally or regularly. Reach out to people you know (e.g., a former roommate) or who have shown an interest in your teen (e.g., a coworker) and invite them to link up with your teen. **Discuss how to establish a friendship** (e.g., suggest inviting the adult over for dinner sometime so that everyone can talk together).

### ♥ CARE ABOUT THE NEIGHBORHOOD

Get to know your neighbors. **Encourage your teen to make a habit of helping people around the neighborhood without expecting payment.** Offering to walk someone's dog or help with the trash is a great way to start a connection. If a neighbor has a hobby or interest in common with your teen, ask if he or she would be willing to meet with your teen to talk about it.

### PARTICIPATE IN A CONGREGATION

For many families, **a great source of positive adult relationships may be through a church, mosque, synagogue, or**

**other faith-based community.** These may include the adults who volunteer in youth activities or the adults you and your teen see during services. Look for mutual interest with these adults who share your values and priorities.

## ENCOURAGE YOUTH PROGRAMS

**Learn about groups in your community that may interest your teen.** Local Boys and Girls Clubs, 4-H, Camp Fire USA, skate parks, theater groups, organized athletic groups, and congregations offer all kinds of programs that are led by trained adults.

## ENSURE SAFETY

Most adults who want to spend time with teens are good people, but unfortunately there is a minority who spend time with teens in order to take advantage of them or to exploit or abuse them. You need to **be cautious about the adults with whom your teen spends time, so take a *balanced* approach,** one that makes sure your daughter or son is connected to caring, responsible adults but also lowers her or his risk of becoming a victim.

It's best to **try to get to know a new person in a group setting first if possible.** You will want other people to be around when your teen and the adult are spending time together. As the relationship continues, check in often with your teen about how it's going. Be alert to any signs of inappropriate behavior. Don't dismiss any reports from your teen, even if what you're hearing seems unimaginable.

## STAY CONNECTED TO OTHERS

*Teens can't have too many responsible, caring adults in their lives—the more, the better. As they grow, form their own identity, and at times perhaps put distance between themselves and their parents, it can be gratifying to know they're connected to safe and supportive adults*

# Dating

*Your Dilemma:*

**"Gavin has mentioned a girl he's seeing. We don't even know what she looks like."**
*or*
**"We're not fond of Jennifer's new boyfriend, Richard. Should we say something?"**

It's a delicate matter to guide teens as they enter the dating world, with its mixed emotions, changing social demands, and strong physical impulses. You may worry that they're too young, that their safety is at stake, that their hearts will be broken. Remember that dating helps teens learn many important life lessons— about caring for themselves and others, communicating with and treating people respectfully, trusting another person, and sharing common interests. They need to know you're there for them and love them enough to set and maintain firm boundaries.

# ⭐ SET FAMILY BOUNDARIES

**The right age to start dating varies from one teen to another and one family to another.** Most teens younger than 14–16, however, do *not* have the social skills necessary to handle dating situations (e.g., can identify and express feelings, be kind to others but also stand up for themselves, recognize dangerous situations). When your teen *is* ready, be sure to *say* **beforehand what you expect and what could happen if he or she doesn't meet those expectations**—whether they're about curfew or balancing the relationship with schoolwork, family time, or other activities.

Many teens feel pressured to go beyond platonic dating and engage in sexual activity, including intercourse, before they are ready. **Share your values about the spectrum of sexual activity and why those values are important to you.** Be specific about what limits of physicality and intimacy you hope your son or daughter will accept.

Help your teen to understand that he or she needn't be in any hurry to engage in sexual intercourse and that doing so can complicate a relationship as well as pose potential consequences. (See pages 53–56 for more information about sexuality.) While you can't control your teen's behavior away from home, **it is possible to influence decisions if he or she clearly understands your values and the reason you hold those values.**

# ☀ ENSURE SAFETY

**Encourage group get-togethers** (e.g., movies, walks), which allow teens a measure of safety and a chance to talk one-on-one at the same time. Also suggest taking dates to public places as a safety precaution.

Decide what you believe about your teen riding in cars with other young, inexperienced drivers. **Insist on seat belts and no**

**drinking and driving.** Talk with your daughter or son about the effects of alcohol and other drugs on people's judgment. **Let your teen know that he or she can always call you for a ride home.**

### ⭐ ENCOURAGE POSITIVE FRIENDSHIPS

**Make it easier for your teens to talk about the people they're interested in.** Regularly and casually ask about what's going on in your daughter's life; remember specific names and events. Enjoy the positive ways dating is affecting your son and compliment him—maybe he's taking showers more regularly! Because teens can feel especially insecure at times, though, avoid teasing and be sympathetic when they take even well-intentioned comments the wrong way.

**To help take the sting out of a breakup, give your teen room to feel bad, but encourage rejoining other friends if he or she is closing off too much.** Other friends help young people maintain their identity and keep the dating relationship in perspective. Suggest counseling if several weeks pass and your son or daughter hasn't rejoined friends.

### ❤️ COMMUNICATE POSITIVELY AS A FAMILY

**Share your own dating experiences** or talk about your first breakup. Showing old school photos can help your son or daughter see that you were young once, too, and experienced some of the same feelings. Seeing the changes in clothes and hairstyles can also provide some comic relief.

**Even if you dislike someone your son or daughter is dating, try to stay neutral.** Negative comments often encourage adolescents to continue a relationship they may actually be growing tired of. If your teen asks what you think of the person, be honest but tactful. **What you think and how you express**

**your concerns matter more than you may realize—and more than your son or daughter may acknowledge.** Better to say calmly, for example, "Ben is so smart, but he doesn't seem to use his smarts in school—why do you think that is?" rather than, "Why are you dating that loser who gets bad grades?"

## ☺ MODEL GOOD RELATIONSHIPS

**Talk with your teen about what traits make a good date or relationship**—qualities such as caring, humor, open communication, equality, playfulness, respect, trust, and reciprocity. Help her or him understand that healthy relationships take effort, even with a really great partner.

### TAKE HEART

*By developing a close relationship with another person, teens can build self-confidence and discover more about who they are. Your guidance can help your teen be safe and keep dating in balance with other aspects of life—while still allowing room to explore and have fun.*

# Sexuality

*Your Dilemma:*

**"Jamal is getting to that age where we think we need to talk to him more about sex, but we're nervous about discussing it."**
*or*
**"I think Mandy is sexually active. What should I do?"**

Your teen is quickly maturing into an adult capable of expressing her or his sexuality—a reality you may try to ignore, but shouldn't. You may vaguely tell your son or daughter what you think he or she needs to know—and hope that will be sufficient. You may even assume teens understand more than they actually do.

In a culture that uses sex to sell everything from beer to movies to pickup trucks, teens especially need clear and loving guidance to develop a healthy, appropriate attitude toward their own sexuality. Help your teen be sure he or she has the information, self-esteem, and restraint to make good choices. Your son or daughter needs more from you than simply to be told, "Just say no."

### 👍 BUILD SELF-ESTEEM

**If teens feel valued for who they are** rather than what they do or who likes them, **they are in a much better position to resist peer pressure and take care of themselves.** Remind your teen that it's okay to be alone at times. By modeling a loving, respectful relationship with your own spouse or partner, you can show your son or daughter that it's possible to create positive relationships even when two people disagree sometimes.

### ❤️ COMMUNICATE POSITIVELY AS A FAMILY

**It's good to have a discussion about physical love *before* any dilemma regarding sexuality comes up** with your teen. Sexual intercourse is a big part of adult sexuality, but it isn't the best choice for teens and it isn't the only way to express intimacy (e.g., hugging, kissing, holding hands). Be candid in discussing sexual matters with your teen, and caution that engaging in sexual intercourse can complicate a relationship as well as pose potential consequences of disease or unplanned pregnancy on future plans, finances, and health.

**Talk with your teen about what boundaries you think are best for her or him and give your reasons why.** Be specific about what limits of physicality and intimacy you hope your teens will respect. For example, you may not approve of your teen and her or his friend making out on the couch or spending time in a bedroom behind closed doors. You may decide the best option is to allow them some alone time in the family room but with doors open.

**Encourage your teen to discuss concerns with you or—if one of you is too uncomfortable—with another trusted adult,** such as a close relative or physician. Keep in mind that confidentiality is important.

### ⭐ KEEP EXPECTATIONS HIGH

Letting your teen know what your expectations are about sexual conduct may actually be a relief for her or him. **When young people know what's expected, they don't have to struggle as much with making all the decisions for themselves.** Research has shown that when parents are clear about their expectations, their teens have fewer unwanted pregnancies.

Remember that restraint in sexual matters can be difficult at any age, but the surging hormones and limited impulse control of adolescence can make it especially tough. Having the desire for physical pleasure is a normal but new feeling for your teen, and he or she needs help handling it. The most helpful thing you can do is to keep the lines of communication open with you or another trusted adult. **Rather than taking a punitive approach after choices you dislike, offer your guidance about what will be a wiser choice in the future.**

If your teen does engage in sexual intercourse, it is appropriate to give honest, complete information about contraception. Sexually active teens need to know that they should talk with their partner first, discuss each other's sexual history, and take precautions to prevent disease and unplanned pregnancy. **It's best if such frank advice can come from adults they trust— not peers who have incomplete or incorrect information.** Remind your son or daughter again about the potential consequences of disease or unplanned pregnancy on future plans, finances, and health.

### CARE ABOUT OTHERS
Talk with your teen about sex as an expression of caring—not just as a way to feel good physically or deal with surging hormones. **Acknowledge the urge to feel good as normal development, but emphasize the importance of the sexual partner** and recognizing that person's safety, self-respect, and limits. At the same time, though, try to help your teen understand that it is also important to take care of herself or himself and not focus on taking care of others by being sexual with them.

### PROVIDE FAMILY SUPPORT
You may find accepting a son's or daughter's growing sexuality difficult enough—you may find accepting homosexuality or being in a cross-racial or cross-cultural relationship even more difficult. Explain whatever concerns you may have, but in the end, try to accept who your teen is. **Make it clear that you will continue to love her or him no matter what.**

### *HONOR EMERGING IDENTITIES*
*In our culture, sex is often a marketing tool, robbing it of much of the reverence and consideration with which it deserves to be treated. By helping teach your teen appropriate ways to explore emerging sexual identities, you can help him or her to become a responsible, caring man or woman.*

# Stress Management

*Your Dilemma:*

**"Nicholas has to give an oral report tomorrow, and he's really stressed out. I don't know how to help him calm down."**

*or*

**"Talisha has been having trouble sleeping. I think something is bothering her."**

Hearing and seeing how stressed your teen may be feeling can be heartbreaking. School, work, sports, and homework, combined with pressures to succeed, to fit in, to care for brothers and sisters, or to make decisions about the future—that's a lot for any teenager to have on her or his mind. Even boredom can bring its own stress.

Your teen may feel like his or her world is falling apart, be unsure where to turn or how to start making things better, react physically by losing or gaining weight or by getting sick, or not even realize he or she is under stress. But that's where you can help: with your guidance, your teen can learn that it's important to pay attention to signs of stress, plan ahead, and know how to relax.

## ♥ COMMUNICATE POSITIVELY AS A FAMILY

When your teen has fears or concerns to discuss with you, be there simply to listen and give support and affection. A lot of stress is caused by change, even positive change, such as a music competition or getting invited to a dance. **Try to head off stress by talking about upcoming changes or events.** Pay attention to signs of stress. **Note what phrases may be popping up when your teen talks,** such as "I'm worried," "freaked out," "overwhelmed," or "swamped."

## 👍 USE PERSONAL POWER

**Help your teen deal with stress by learning to recognize her or his best stress-reducing strategies, even if they're different from your way of relaxing** (e.g., listening to music louder than you would). Physical activity and playing with a pet are great ways to rid tension. Writing about feelings or reading a book can also provide comfort, as can meditation, yoga, or praying.

## ☺ PLAN AHEAD AND MAKE THOUGHTFUL DECISIONS

Encourage your teen to think ahead about the day's schedule. Does your son need to prepare for a quiz? Has your daughter started the project that's due next week? Using a to-do list or **setting daily goals is an excellent way to reduce stress**—and provides a sense of control and accomplishment.

## Signs of Stress

Physical signs of stress are often mistaken as an illness. If you think your teen is suffering from stress, look for some of these symptoms:

| Physical Symptoms | Psychological Symptoms |
|---|---|
| Nausea, dizziness | Lack of concentration |
| Headaches, stomachaches | Forgetfulness, carelessness |
| Loss of/or increased appetite (weight gain or loss) | Decrease in school performance |
| Rashes, dry mouth | Inability to study |
| Nail or lip biting | Irritability |
| Fatigue, sweating | Nightmares |
| Increase in illness | Boredom |
| Rapid heart rate, shaking | Withdrawal |
| Frequent urination | Sadness or depression |

If stress is interfering too much with your teen's day-to-day well-being, help her or him find a counselor, psychologist, or psychiatrist.

## USE TIME CONSTRUCTIVELY

**Chances are your teen deals with stress on the basis of what he or she has seen you do.** Maintain your health with habits that keep stress away in the first place: exercise regularly, eat healthy foods, and get enough sleep.

Also take a look at what choices everyone in the family is

making and decide whether you need to slow down and spend some time at home unwinding. Sometimes parents and teens may need to evaluate and **let go of things that are good and positive but only adding stress.**

## MINIMIZE STRESS

*By giving your teen the tools to work through anxious feelings and responses to get to laughter and excitement, you can help her or him learn how to enjoy more peace and fulfillment in life.*

# Self-Acceptance

*Your Dilemma:*

**"LaKeisha walks around with her head down most of the time. She can hardly look other people in the eye."**
*or*
**"Jamie studied all night and still got a D on his history test. He came home and said, 'I can't do anything right.' "**

Striving daily to feel happy, loved, and accepted for who you are is part of everyone's life. But for teens, feeling good about who they are can be particularly difficult given all the expectations and pressures from parents, siblings, peers, teachers, and others in their life, as well as so many often-unrealistic ideals from popular culture.

How you demonstrate your acceptance of your teen plays a big role in her or his self-image. Even if they don't look like models, perform like super athletes, or get straight As, young people can learn ways to boost their feelings about themselves.

### BUILD SELF-ESTEEM

To help teens discover specific ways to boost how they feel about themselves, **parents can point out the positive side of their personality traits.** For example, a thought such as, "I'm too emotional" can be seen as, "I'm in touch with my feelings." Have your son or daughter list past successes, whether big or small, and look over this list periodically.

**Write your teen notes, too, every so often, and comment on specific qualities that make you proud—and not just after major accomplishments.** Don't assume he or she knows how you feel. For example, you might say, "You were brave to go first in your group presentation," "You've worked hard to bring your math grade up," or "You're great at asking sharp questions." Even if teens act as though they don't want to hear this, almost everyone appreciates genuine praise. When you need to comment on behavior you don't like, be clear that it is just the behavior with which you are unhappy.

### ENCOURAGE POSITIVE FRIENDSHIPS

Ask teens about their friends: "Are they good students?" "Do they encourage you?" "Can you confide in them?" "What do you like to do together?" "Does the relationship feel reciprocal?" **Encourage your daughter or son to stick with friends who are uplifting and supportive,** not negative, draining, or who put her or him down. Invite supportive friends to join the family for pizza. When you hear kids and their friends talking negatively about others, call them on it and help them find the positive side.

### ♥ PROVIDE FAMILY SUPPORT

Show your support for your teen's interests. Attend games and performances. **Even if you can't make the entire event, just showing up for some of it can mean a lot to a young person.** Participate in school events. Display her or his art and awards. **Respect your teen's boundaries, too.** If he or she doesn't want you to show a lot of affection, keep in mind that a brief touch on the arm or back can express a lot.

### ♥ COMMUNICATE POSITIVELY AS A FAMILY

When teens talk, show interest. **To get them to elaborate, ask some specific questions:** "Tell me three good things that happened today," "Tell me something you wish you could change about your day," or "What was the funniest thing that happened this week?" Talk about your day and what's on your mind.

### ☀ HELP YOUR COMMUNITY APPRECIATE YOUNG PEOPLE

**Find ways to help your community value young people instead of regarding them as a problem.** Schools, neighborhoods, congregations, and businesses can all become places where teens have the opportunity to voice their opinions, help others, and build self-esteem. Help create leadership roles for teens in the community, such as youth advisory councils within local government or at your congregation. Ask a local restaurant or coffee shop to exhibit student art, or encourage your school to set up a mentoring program.

## BE ACCEPTING

*If teens can accept who they are, imperfections and all, they'll have the confidence to take reasonable risks and approach life openly and enthusiastically. With your guidance and encouragement, your daughter or son will set goals that are realistic and find ways to reach those goals.*

# Anger Management

*Your Dilemma:*

**"Mei just blows up when she's upset. She yells at me, and sometimes I wind up yelling back."**
*or*
**"Door slamming. That's what Nate does when he's mad. He doesn't speak to us, but he slams doors."**

Anger is a normal emotion, especially during adolescence, when great hormonal and physical changes are occurring. Anger can also be a mask for depression, substance abuse, insecurity, or unresolved grief. Most of us know firsthand that an inability to express anger respectfully can make talking with others difficult, if not impossible, and hurt relationships.

When their tempers flare, teens may say things they don't mean, and if they recognize what they've said and then pretend otherwise, they may feel even worse. By discussing expectations with your teen about respectful behavior and self-control and by modeling positive ways to handle your own anger, you can help your son or daughter learn how to keep cool, express this important emotion appropriately, and feel better.

## USE PERSONAL POWER

To help your teen avoid unnecessary anger in the first place, **encourage her or him to take responsibility for preventing conflict situations.** For example, if your teen doesn't like her 10-year-old sister reading her diary and they share a bedroom, encourage your teen not to leave the diary where it's visible.

**Teach your teen to consider whether some angry thoughts are overgeneralizations and to try to change negative thoughts to positive thoughts.** Gently point out use of words such as *never* or *always*. Or later, after the heat of the moment has passed, help him or her to reflect on how things did occur. If, for example, your teen can reflect truthfully about an angry statement, such as, "You're never home on the weekends," he or she may realize that you are home most weekends, but that he or she is wanting more of your attention.

## COMMUNICATE POSITIVELY AS A FAMILY

Let your teen know that anger is normal and that finding ways to express it constructively strengthens relationships. **Discuss how you as a family handle anger and how you as a family could handle anger better.** Talk about how your own parents and siblings handled anger when you were a teen. Here are some questions you may want to ask: "What makes you angry?" "What goes on in your mind when you're angry?" "Do you think girls tend to suppress their anger more than boys? If so, why?" or "What happens if you don't express your anger?"

## ☺ RESOLVE CONFLICTS PEACEFULLY

**Share ideas with your teen about what to do when he or she recognizes feeling angry.** Explain that it first helps to admit you're angry with someone. Choosing to disagree for the moment, or to take a break, a walk, a shower, or some other activity can help diffuse the anger and help you to calm down. Then you can think more clearly about what's going on and decide if you want to take some action and in what way, or do nothing.

## ✷ BE A ROLE MODEL

Even when you are angry at your teen, speak respectfully. Use a variety of words, such as *irritated*, *annoyed*, or *frustrated*, to model for your teen the range of feelings that anger can take.

---

### Tips for Expressing Anger

To help your teen learn how to constructively express anger, share these tips—preferably at a time when everyone is calm:

◆ Use "I" statements to express your feelings. Avoid blaming the other person (e.g., instead of "You're never on time," you could say, "I feel as though I have to wait for you a lot").

◆ Stick to the current issue. Avoid bringing up past events.

◆ Avoid qualifying a "yes" with a "but."

◆ Focus on solutions rather than accusations.

**If your teen yells or speaks disrespectfully, it's important to communicate that such behavior is not acceptable** and does not help resolve anger or a problem. If your teen screams, "I hate you," redirect the emotion by saying, "You really mean you're angry at me. Please don't say *hate*. And remember that I love you no matter how angry you are at me." Don't react if he or she says it again. You might simply walk away after calmly responding, and resume the conversation when everyone is less tense.

## FIND THE CALM

*The naturally powerful and raw response that anger can evoke can easily complicate your teen's day-to-day world. By talking positively and respectfully to everyone, you and your teen can together appreciate the importance of expressing anger and doing so in a way that keeps life calmer and more harmonious.*

# Depression

*Your Dilemma:*

**"First Allison's tearful, then she's short-tempered. It's been like this for a month. Is this just a 'phase'?"**

*or*

**"Steve seems to sleep all the time lately whenever he's home. He doesn't wash his hair, eat much, or call his friends. What can we do?"**

Sorting out whether your teen is sad or depressed can take a careful eye—and may require the help of a trained mental health professional. Depression is a serious medical illness that negatively affects how you feel, the way you think, and how you act; it can cause an overwhelming sense of despair. It's normal to feel sad in response to stressful events or losses, and in such situations people may describe themselves as feeling "depressed"; however, sadness and depression are different. Feelings of sadness will lessen with time, but depression can continue for months, even years. If left untreated, depression puts a person at risk of suicide.

Fortunately, many people who have depression respond well to a variety of treatments, including counseling, medications, and other types of therapy. If your teen is struggling with depression, it is essential to get help right away and to create an atmosphere of hope.

### ♥ COMMUNICATE POSITIVELY AS A FAMILY

If you suspect your teen is depressed, don't hesitate to ask about her or his frame of mind. If your teen refuses to acknowledge being depressed, **express your concern and the importance of getting some reassurance or help,** including a professional evaluation. Try to calmly explain that an aspect of the illness is difficulty in acknowledging feelings.

Reassure your teen that depression is treatable. Make a point to spend time together, without expecting her or him to be cheerful. **Keep in mind: depression is an illness, not a character flaw—it's no one's fault.** Learn about depression and its symptoms. Request information from your physician or a counselor, and share what you learn with family members and others who care about your teen. If your teen receives a prescription for medication to treat depression, be sure you and your teen understand the dosage requirements, side effects, and how long it takes to start experiencing results.

### ⊞ CREATE A SAFE, CARING SCHOOL

**Make sure your teen's school staff is aware of her or his depression so that they can provide additional support.** If the staff seem uninformed about depression, talk to the admin-

## Symptoms of Depression

Teens may not always act like it, but they really need to know that parents are paying attention to what's going on with them. If your teen experiences five or more of the following symptoms* for at least two consecutive weeks in addition to showing a loss of interest or pleasure in usual activities and persistent feelings of sadness or anxiety, don't wait to see if your teen "snaps out of it"—seek professional help right away:

♦ Changes in appetite that have caused weight loss or gain not related to dieting.

♦ Loss of energy or increased fatigue.

♦ Trouble sleeping or oversleeping.

♦ Restlessness or irritability.

♦ Feeling worthless or inappropriately guilty.

♦ Trouble thinking, concentrating, or making decisions.

♦ Thinking about death and suicide or having a plan to commit suicide.

*Symptoms from the American Psychiatric Association Web site accessed January 22, 2004: www.psych.org/public_info/depression.cfm.

istration about training staff and parents on depression in adolescents. Be careful about respecting your teen's confidence and dignity.

### PROMOTE A POSITIVE FUTURE

Don't expect teens who are depressed to "cheer up" or do something just because you ask or you're upbeat; part of the illness is difficulty in doing things. But **you can take your**

**son or daughter places and help find things to look forward to or goals to set.** It's important to remind your teen that you believe in her or his ability to focus on positive events.

### BUILD SELF-ESTEEM

If your teen feels up to it, ask if he or she will help you in some type of service to others. **Volunteering to help others can be a great boost to self-esteem,** and sometimes engaging in an activity can become a welcome distraction.

### ENCOURAGE RELATIONSHIPS WITH OTHER ADULTS

Ask a trusted relative, friend, or neighbor to spend time with your teen doing something easy together, such as going to a movie. **Support from others and a willingness to listen can mean a lot.**

### *SHOW YOU CARE*

*It isn't easy to take care of a daughter or son who is struggling with the painful experience of depression. Be generous with encouragement. Help your teen recognize that depression is an illness that does not diminish her or his worth in any way.*

# Jobs Outside the Home

*Your Dilemma:*

**"Melanie's grades have dropped since last semester; last term, she wasn't working more than 20 hours a week."**

*or*

**"Tran wants a stereo, but we think he should earn it. Should we ask him to get a job?"**

Having a part-time job can teach your teen many valuable skills: responsibility, time management, and getting along with other people are just a few. But each young person's situation and abilities are unique. Some teens can handle a full academic schedule, involvement in extracurricular activities, and a job. Others can't—at least not yet. Help your son or daughter weigh carefully the benefits against the drawbacks.

## ⭐ SET FAMILY BOUNDARIES

Whether your family needs the additional income of your teen working or he or she wants some extra spending money, be sure the job schedule allows enough time for home, schoolwork, and other obligations. **Limit the job to no more than 15 hours per week.** Adolescents who work more than this tend to do poorly in school and are deprived of much-needed sleep. Check community curfews and local labor laws to ensure that employers are not taking advantage of the hours your teen works.

## ❤ COMMUNICATE POSITIVELY AS A FAMILY

Check in with your teen to **make sure the location, hours, workplace, and type of work are safe and suitable.** Is the job likely to benefit her or his self-esteem? **Regularly ask your teen how work is going,** how he or she is getting along with supervisors and coworkers, and whether the work is enjoyable. Talking with kids about their jobs helps them make the most of what they learn from their work experience.

## ☺ PLAN AHEAD AND MAKE THOUGHTFUL DECISIONS

Help your teen learn how to manage time. You might spend some time at the beginning of each week discussing everyone's schedule for the coming week. **Talk to your teen about how to make the best use of her or his paychecks.** Demonstrate how to create a budget, set up a savings account, and balance a checkbook, and encourage giving to others in need.

## 🧭 TAKE PERSONAL RESPONSIBILITY

**Teens don't learn as well when parents rescue them from their own mistakes** (e.g., by giving them rides to work more than once when their own poor planning makes them late). Letting your child face the consequences of his or her actions is an effective way to teach responsible behavior.

**If your son or daughter starts a job and wants to quit, discuss why he or she feels this way.** If the decision seems ungrounded, try to find ways to inspire him or her to stick with the job. Sometimes, it's important for your teen to hang on to one job while looking for another. If the reason is valid, help your teen plan how best to communicate her or his decision to a supervisor.

## FIND A SENSE OF PURPOSE
**Talk to your teen about whether the job contributes to a sense of purpose in life and builds a sense of self or is "just a job."** You might ask: "What kind of job would provide you the greatest sense of accomplishment?" "Is service to others a part of the picture, or is making money the main objective?" Remind your son or daughter that opportunities to help others, to provide good service, and to be part of a team can make even the most repetitive job worthwhile.

## AIM FOR AN INDEPENDENT LIFE
*Having a job as a teenager can provide valuable life experience beyond family and school. By earning a regular paycheck now, teens can begin to see that they'll be able to provide for themselves when they make the move to living independently.*

# Money

*Your Dilemma:*

**"Even though she gets an allowance,
Becca ends up asking for more cash
by the end of the week."**
*or*
**"Justin has a job and earns his own money, but
he spends it all on magazines and junk food."**

Despite the significance of money in the world, relatively few high schools—or parents—teach teens about how to *handle* money. It's important to recognize how your own attitudes about money affect the way you live, the choices you make, perhaps even your feelings about your own worth—and that you likely pass on these attitudes to your teen.

If you're completely at ease with all matters financial, consider yourself fortunate. In this case, sharing your skills and knowledge with your children is a matter of priority. On the other hand, if financial matters have always been confusing or something you'd rather not discuss, helping your kids understand financial realities tends to be stickier. Regardless, you can boost your teen's ability to handle money responsibly and make it a positive aspect of life.

### ♥ COMMUNICATE POSITIVELY AS A FAMILY

If you can talk about money frankly, it, like most difficult topics, becomes less mysterious. **Include money in regular family discussions, both specifically** (e.g., the price of movie tickets) **and generally** (e.g., the importance of recognizing whether advertising makes us want items we don't need). Encourage your teen to make her or his choices about spending money independently of media persuasion.

### MAINTAIN INTEGRITY

**Be honest about your own attitudes regarding money.** For important purchases, such as cars and vacations, get your teen's input. Talk together about how you come to your decisions. If you're in debt or on financial assistance, explain how this works and your plans for moving ahead.

### COMMIT TO LEARNING

**Often, tackling the emotional component of dealing with money is harder for a parent than learning the practical skills.** Consider learning some practical skills by taking a money-management class, reading books, or consulting financial experts. Know that your willingness to explore this terrain will set a powerful example for your teen.

## Questions to Help Discuss Money Matters

To help your family talk frankly about financial issues, consider these questions together:

♦ How do you feel about money? How important is money? When is money not the most important thing?

♦ How does the way you spend money reflect your values? Is charitable giving a core part of managing money along with earning and saving?

♦ What money or other resources do you need to achieve your personal or family goals?

♦ Do you consider yourself a smart consumer? Why or why not?

♦ How often do you buy something impulsively?

♦ Do you think credit cards are a good idea? Why or why not?

♦ When you think about earning money now or in the future, do you focus more on how much you want to earn or how you want to earn it? Why?

### VALUE YOUTH

**Encourage others to help your teen learn about finances.** Work with your teen's teachers or the parent organization at her or his school to offer an age-appropriate personal-finance course. See if your local bank would give a free money-management seminar to teens from your neighborhood. Perhaps some businesses would match their savings (e.g., up to $25 each) to enable them to open an account.

### ☺ PLAN AHEAD AND MAKE THOUGHTFUL DECISIONS

To help your teen appreciate what your family has at home and what it will take to be out on her or his own, **work out a family budget.** Your daughter or son doesn't need to know every detail of your finances, but it's important to teach an awareness of basic expenses. Demonstrate what it's like to be in charge of family expenses by inviting your teen to pay the bills with you for a month.

**Emphasize the importance of starting a savings account,** and encourage your teen to think about setting aside savings weekly or monthly. **Carefully explain credit card use** and the risks of interest rates, late payment fees, and letting a balance add up versus paying the total bill monthly.

## *INVEST SOUNDLY*

*Regardless of the path your teen chooses in life, he or she needs your help in learning how to manage money competently and confidently. By fostering an understanding of the choices people have about money, you can help your child learn to better enjoy what he or she has, spend wisely, and save for the future.*

# Appearance

*Your Dilemma:*

**"Honey! Your hair! It's pink!"**

**"Magenta. And it's only the tips."**

**"Right. Magenta. Interesting effect."**

**"I knew you'd be like this."**

Body piercing, tattoos, dramatic hairstyles, and unconventional clothing are all part of youth culture. For many teens, exotic attire is an important part of their emerging personal identity. So where is the line between healthy self-expression and bizarrely antisocial behavior? How do you set reasonable limits yet leave room for each teen's unique personality? By being honest about your own reactions and defining clear boundaries for your teen, it's possible to come up with some useful guidelines for what's okay—

while respecting and supporting your daughter's or son's individuality.

### ♥ COMMUNICATE POSITIVELY AS A FAMILY

**Whatever your teen's new look, consider that it may simply be an attempt to fit in with peers.** Listen without judgment to what she or he tells you. Fashion is a matter of taste, and you don't all have to agree on what looks good. Recognize that part of what your daughter or son is doing is defining separation from you, which is part of growing up.

**Be creative when discussing changes that are more or less permanent,** such as tattoos or piercings. For example, ask your teen, "Imagine if I got that tattoo—would it be weird for someone my age to have that?" If they answer yes, you can respond, "Well, someday you'll be my age." Another approach is to ask your son or daughter to consider a trend that was popular six months ago and ask if he or she still likes it. The answer is often no. Sometimes, it's easier to get teens to think about the past rather than imagining their future tastes.

### ☀ ENSURE SAFETY

**Make sure your teen understands that some fashion trends can be risky or even dangerous.** In general, procedures that involve puncturing the skin (such as piercing and tattooing) carry the risk of infection and, if performed carelessly, transmission of disease. **You may want to set a minimum age at which your teen can choose certain styles.** (Or, this type of adornment may simply be unacceptable to you.)

### ★ SET FAMILY BOUNDARIES

**If you don't like your teen's new look, reflect on why.** Does it not fit your style and your "image"? Or does the concern deal with values and safety? To help everyone understand what really matters, consider whether the mode of dress or adornment in question is:

◆ Safe, or involves a possible health risk.

◆ More or less permanent.

◆ Sexually inappropriate (skintight, skimpy, or otherwise suggestive clothing can put young people—especially girls—at risk for sexual aggression and exploitation).

◆ Gender bending (e.g., boys now color their hair and wear earrings).

◆ Offensive (e.g., T-shirt slogans that use profanity or advertise illegal substances).

◆ A sign of allegiance to a particular group or gang.

◆ Prohibited by your teen's school.

◆ Likely to affect your teen's employment status.

**Discuss your boundaries with your teen** and give her or him the chance to tell you what she or he thinks of the fairness of these limits. **Be flexible on the ones that aren't harmful or permanent**—after all, pink hair can be brown again tomorrow.

### BUILD SELF-ESTEEM
**Emphasize your teen's positive character traits**— honesty, kindness, intelligence, creativity, humor—**rather than appearance or your embarrassment or criticism of her or him.** If you see that your daughter or son is basing self-worth on desirability, and is extremely preoccupied with sexually alluring fashion, **discuss the difference between dressing attractively and dressing provocatively.**

## *LOVE THEM NO MATTER HOW THEY LOOK*

*Even if you don't like the way your teen dresses or adorns himself or herself, be sure to offer your love and respectful regard. Do your best to see past whatever bothers you and to recognize his or her genuine inner beauty. With your support, your son or daughter will more easily develop a strong and healthy personal identity.*

# Body Image

*Your Dilemma:*

**"Abby's always asking how she looks in something. 'Mom, does this dress make my butt look too big!' 'Does this sweater make me look fat?'"**

*or*

**"Our son is pretty thin. Steve is worried that he's going to be the scrawniest boy in class."**

The pressure to conform to certain ideals of beauty can be a struggle at any age. But for your teen, who has yet to fully develop a strong sense of personal identity and whose body is changing rapidly, her or his size and shape can become a source of great anxiety. With the entertainment, advertising, news, and fashion industries promoting images of people with "perfect" hair, teeth, skin, figures, and clothes, it's easy to understand why your teen may feel inadequate about how she or he looks and insecure about other aspects of who she or he is. By encouraging teens to cultivate a strong sense of self-worth, parents can help them learn to see beyond the mirror.

### BUILD SELF-ESTEEM

It's good to compliment your teen occasionally about how nice he or she looks. Excessively emphasizing appearance, however—even a lot of positive comments—can foster a great deal of self-consciousness. **Emphasize your teen's positive character traits and abilities, rather than how attractive he or she is.**

### BE A ROLE MODEL

Pay attention to your own attitudes about physical appearance. If you are preoccupied with your own weight or appearance, your teen is likely to internalize these attitudes. Try to **develop and express a greater acceptance of how you look.**

### COMMUNICATE POSITIVELY AS A FAMILY

To **help your teen see how views of body image and weight together affect people's self-esteem,** ask if he or she thinks people who are overweight receive the same treatment as those who are thin. Ask your teen about his or her own biases about weight. Point out that you can find numerous different types of shampoo, toothpaste, salad dressings, and other items at the store, but magazines and the media emphasize only one body type as the ideal. **Encourage your daughter or son to recognize that there are many ways to be beautiful or handsome.**

## ♥ PROVIDE FAMILY SUPPORT

Encourage your teen to be physically active. Regular exercise offers countless health and appearance benefits. Spend time together outdoors as a family, or if you enjoy a particular activity, teach it to your son or daughter. **Emphasize the importance of being and feeling strong and healthy.**

**If your teen tries to achieve some ideal body image by** overexercising, overusing body-building supplements, taking nonprescription steroids, or developing **destructive** eating **habits** (not eating or throwing up after eating), **get professional help** from a counselor experienced with eating disorders and related issues. Consult your family physician if you are unsure where to turn for help.

## ⭐ ENCOURAGE POSITIVE FRIENDSHIPS

If your teen's friends are overly concerned about their clothes, dieting, and other people's appearance, it might be difficult for your teen to feel at ease about body image and free to be who he or she is. **Remind your teen that there are a lot of forms of beauty and handsomeness, and what's most attractive about most people is the energy and personality that shine through.** Help your teen understand that he or she doesn't have to look a certain way.

## *LIKING WHAT'S IN THE MIRROR*

*It's natural to want to be attractive; you can't expect your daughter or son not to. But parents can help teens recognize their own genuine worth so that regardless of how little they conform to a certain beauty ideal, they can look in the mirror and like what they see.*

# Separation/Divorce

*Your Dilemma:*

**"Lamar is upset because he's heard his mom and me arguing, but I don't know how much I should tell him."**
*or*
**"My daughter keeps asking me for reassurance when I don't know what's going to happen. She's acting insecure and moody, and I'm worried about her."**

One of the most difficult aspects of parenting is being called upon to help and comfort your child when you feel least capable of doing so. This challenge is seldom more painful than when you're going through a separation or divorce. The strain and emotional trauma can leave you feeling exhausted, confused, angry, scared, heartbroken, and depressed—sometimes all at once.

In the midst of all that, you may look into your teen's worried face and feel the last trace of your composure crumble. The pain written there is plain to see, but there *are* things you can do to ease your teen's hurt and grief. Draw strength and support wherever you can find it, and pass it along. Kids can learn from seeing adults face and deal with their problems and emotions.

### ♥ PROVIDE FAMILY SUPPORT

Maintain familiar routines as much as possible. **Keep going to your teen's events** even if you feel like staying away because you don't want to run into someone who might ask how you're doing.

**Teens need to understand that they are not alone in what they may be feeling.** Suggest that your son or daughter read about other teens' experiences with divorce. Books written by kids for kids whose parents divorce are available at the library and bookstore. Say more often that you love her or him.

### ♥ COMMUNICATE POSITIVELY AS A FAMILY

Spare your teen unnecessary pain. **Avoid speaking harshly about your former or separated spouse or partner to your teen, however angry you may be.** Find other places to express these feelings (e.g., with a friend, a counselor, or in a journal). Your teen will also be more likely to talk to you about certain problems if he or she knows you're not going to criticize the other parent.

**If your teen does come to you with a problem about the other parent, acknowledge the situation and try to emphasize the positive** (as long as the problem does not involve a safety concern). You might say, "I understand what you're saying. I've experienced similar concerns and frustrations, but your father/mother has many wonderful qualities, and I'm sure he/she loves you very much."

**Remember that you can't "fix" your teen's feelings.** You can listen supportively and say how important his or her feelings are to you. When teens receive encouragement to *feel* what they feel, they learn to trust their feelings and their ability to express themselves. When you offer compassion without judgment, you make it easier for your son or daughter to move on.

## ☺ MODEL GOOD RELATIONSHIPS

Don't hesitate to lean on your network of support. Let your friends and loved ones remind you what a good person you are. Reach out if you find your safety net is small. If there's a neighbor who's always seemed friendly, invite her or him for coffee, not necessarily to talk about your problems, but to start making connections. Join a support group for people going through divorce or seek professional help if problems feel bigger. **Talking with others in a similar situation can be reassuring,** and new friendships can blossom.

## BUILD SELF-ESTEEM

Take extra care of yourself during this time so that you're better able to help your teen cope with the changes at home. And **when your teen sees that you are taking care of yourself, he or she won't feel responsible for taking care of you.** Reassure your teen that he or she is not to blame for this situation or expected to keep your spirits up.

## DO YOUR BEST

*A separation or divorce can be especially wrenching when kids are involved. But if your teen sees you face the turmoil maturely, you will send the message that you're doing your best and that things really will get better.*

# Single Parenting

*Your Dilemma:*

**"Kira has mono and needs a lot of care right now. She resents it when I go to work."**

*or*

**"Every time my daughter and I have a conflict, she gets nasty toward me and threatens to live just at her dad's."**

Regardless of how you became a single parent (e.g., by choice, divorce, abandonment, due to a death), feelings of grief, hurt, or fear about how to manage alone can be overwhelming at times—as they can for your teen. If your spouse or partner has died or you've separated or divorced, your teen has his or her own sorrow and confusing emotions. If your son or daughter hasn't known a father or a mother, they may wonder why.

As challenging as it may be, as one parent you can still give your teen what he or she needs—without trying to be both mother and father. By focusing on how to make the best of circumstances, you're likely to discover strengths you didn't know you had if you previously relied on someone else—and your teen will learn from you. Raised by one parent, your daughter or son has an even greater opportunity to make real contributions to the family and to learn much about her or his own worth and abilities.

### TAKE PERSONAL RESPONSIBILITY

As hard as it is, try to accept that you cannot change how your teen may be feeling and avoid trying to reason him or her out of it. **If you validate feelings, he or she is more likely to talk to you,** trust you, and accept your choices, especially when you may be ready to introduce a date or new friend.

### VALUE YOUTH

**You needn't take on all the work at home alone, but be careful not to lean too much on your teen.** He or she also is tackling many developmental issues of adolescence. Find appropriate ways to share typical responsibilities. Invite your son to help make decisions about chores. Teach your daughter about budgeting by involving her in the process. **Show that you value what your teen can do.**

### ENCOURAGE RELATIONSHIPS WITH OTHER ADULTS

The stress of single parenting may make you feel like withdrawing and isolating yourself. Instead, **try to reach out and stay engaged in positive activities with other adults.** Call on them to help in specific ways. Get to know neighbors and the parents of your teen's friends or join a group or parenting class for single parents of teens. Teens need to feel that there are a number of safe adults (e.g., a trusted friend, relatives, or mentor) who care about them or share a common interest with them; encourage your daughter or son to spend time with those adults. If you're feeling overwhelmed, consult a professional therapist; a good counselor can serve as a helpful "coach" as your family is moving through tough times.

## USE PERSONAL POWER

Even if you long for a parenting partner, **try to avoid idealizing dual parenting, especially in front of your teen.** Keep in mind that no situation is perfect: many couples don't discover they have conflicting parenting styles until after they've had kids, and many parents feel alone even with a partner. **Focus on the assets of single parenting,** such as the benefits of making decisions without compromising, or learning to make your own decisions. **Help your teen to adopt a positive attitude about what's possible rather than focus on what's missing.**

## PROVIDE FAMILY SUPPORT

If your teen's other parent plays a part in your teen's life, **respect your son's or daughter's need to spend time with the other parent.** Resist making negative comments about that person, competing for your teen's love, or using your teen to spy.

## SINGLE, BUT NOT ALONE

*If you can relax and take pride as a single parent, you will be better able to make sure your teen gets what he or she needs, even if the other parent is not in the picture. By modeling how to turn what may be seen as a disadvantage into an empowering experience, you will teach your teen how to better manage difficulties that come her or his way.*

# Race and Ethnicity

*Your Dilemma:*

**"Our neighborhood isn't very diverse. I'd like Ian to be comfortable around people of backgrounds different from our own."**

*or*

**"I don't think Maria appreciates her ethnic heritage."**

Regardless of your own racial and cultural heritage—whether you're Asian, American Indian, Aboriginal, Arab, Hispanic, Black, White, or multiracial—race is a mix of celebration and tension in modern life. Race and culture undeniably influence where you live and work, or where your teen goes to school, who your friends are, and how you perceive the world and the people in it.

Whatever attitudes and beliefs about race and culture you hold, your teen is likely to carry them on into the world. Are they values worthy of handing down? One of the greatest gifts you can give your teen is the belief in her or his own ability to help create a fair and equal society.

### BE HONEST

**Be honest about your own feelings**, but create an atmosphere in which your teen can speak freely. **Be honest about other people:** help your teen understand that we aren't all the same, but others' experiences and viewpoints do matter.

### COMMUNICATE POSITIVELY AS A FAMILY

**If your teen says or does something that supports a bias or stereotype, point it out:** "Why is that joke funny?" Express your concern and explain why. Encourage your teen to think about how it would feel or how it has felt when someone has made fun of her or him.

### UPHOLD EQUALITY AND SOCIAL JUSTICE

While group identity is critical for teens, **they need to learn that pride** in your own group or allegiance to others "just like you" **doesn't mean disrespect for others or putting others down to promote yourself.** Help your teen identify stereotypes. Ask how they're depicted in movies, ads, and other media and elsewhere, and what messages they send about race, culture, religion, gender roles, and socioeconomic backgrounds.

**Help your teen look for ways to get actively involved in social change.** Encourage your daughter to contribute part of her allowance or earnings to a cause she supports. Work with your son's school to help students start a campaign for peace.

# Rate Your Cultural Competence

How culturally aware are you? With your teen, rate yourselves using the chart below (type of contact: weekly, monthly, yearly, rarely, or never).

|  | w | m | y | r | n |
|---|---|---|---|---|---|
| I see people from a variety of cultures in my neighborhood. | ❏ | ❏ | ❏ | ❏ | ❏ |
| I see people from a variety of cultures in my community. | ❏ | ❏ | ❏ | ❏ | ❏ |
| I talk to people with cultural backgrounds different from mine. | ❏ | ❏ | ❏ | ❏ | ❏ |
| I watch TV shows that positively portray people from a variety of cultures. | ❏ | ❏ | ❏ | ❏ | ❏ |
| I listen to music from cultures other than my own. | ❏ | ❏ | ❏ | ❏ | ❏ |
| I eat foods from cultures other than my own. | ❏ | ❏ | ❏ | ❏ | ❏ |
| I study in school about people from different cultures. | ❏ | ❏ | ❏ | ❏ | ❏ |
| I read positive stories about people from different cultures. | ❏ | ❏ | ❏ | ❏ | ❏ |
| I attend events that celebrate different cultures. | ❏ | ❏ | ❏ | ❏ | ❏ |
| I treat people as individuals, not just as members of a group. | ❏ | ❏ | ❏ | ❏ | ❏ |

## MAINTAIN INTEGRITY

If your teen becomes the target of bias, don't minimize the experience. **Encourage her or him to speak up** (e.g., to say "I'm not going to listen to you" when discriminated against)—for others as well. **Reassure your teen that there is nothing "wrong" with her or him,** that he or she is a good person.

**If your teen is wondering if he or she has been treated unfairly, encourage your son or daughter to reflect on a few questions:** "How did I compare to others in the same situation?" "Was the outcome based on experience, attitude, ability, or education? Or on race, religion, sex, or age?"

## PROMOTE CULTURAL COMPETENCE

**The more teens know about different races and cultures and their own, the more comfortable they will be in all kinds of situations.** Talk about your family's cultural background and experiences and how these have affected your lives. Encourage your teen to have friends from diverse cultures. Serve dishes at meals from other cultures, and listen to music from cultures other than your own.

## CREATE A CARING WORLD

*Despite many doors that have opened over the decades, racism and social injustice continue to hurt many individuals. As a parent, you can help teach your teen to take responsibility in whatever way he or she can to help remedy the suffering.*

# Substance Use and Abuse

*Your Dilemma:*

**"We want to talk to Toby about drugs
and drinking, but we also want him
to know that we trust him."**

*or*

**"Faye has been avoiding us lately and won't go
on family outings anymore. She doesn't seem
like herself. We're worried she's using drugs."**

You may find it hard to believe that your teen would
ever drink alcohol or use other drugs. Or if you grew
up in the 60s and 70s, you may feel hypocritical telling
your daughter or son not to do things you did yourself
at that age. The topic can be upsetting and emotionally charged, but by avoiding a discussion about it,
you do your teen a disservice. Your son or daughter
needs a great deal of guidance and support to make
wise choices.

**★ ENCOURAGE POSITIVE FRIENDSHIPS**

**Research strongly suggests that peer influence affects rates of substance use.** Get to know your teens' friends. If you notice that they have a positive effect on your teen, say so: "You always seem happy when Sarah's around." If certain friends seem to bring out negative attitudes and behaviors, carefully express your concerns and set limits on how much time your teen may spend with them.

**★ KEEP EXPECTATIONS HIGH**

**Acknowledge that your teen may want to experiment** with using alcohol and other drugs out of curiosity, to seem more grown-up, to rebel, to deal with shyness, or for other reasons, **but emphasize that alcohol use is illegal under age 21**

---

## Underage Drinking

According to the American Medical Association,* underage drinking:

◆ Is a factor in nearly half of all teen automobile crashes—the leading cause of death among teens;

◆ Contributes to youth suicides, fatal injuries, and homicides—the next three leading causes of death for teens after auto accidents;

◆ Is linked to two-thirds of all sexual assaults and date rapes of teens and college students; and

◆ Is a major factor in unprotected sex among teens.

*Share this information with your kids.*

*Statistics reported by the American Medical Association Web site accessed January 28, 2004: www.ama-assn.org/ama/pub/category/print/3557.html.

and describe the potential serious consequences of any drug use (e.g., addictive properties, impairment of judgment and the risk of getting arrested). Be specific with your teen about your expectations regarding alcohol and other drugs. Make it clear that you believe in his or her ability to live a successful life and that you trust her or him to make good choices.

## ⬟ SET FAMILY BOUNDARIES

Even if your teen smokes marijuana or drinks alcohol "just once," removing certain privileges (e.g., driving) as previously agreed may be an appropriate consequence. **A seemingly isolated incident may signify something's not going right.** Perhaps your teen isn't feeling valued or is having trouble fitting in at school. If you can inquire about the incident respectfully, you create a valuable opportunity to help get her or his life back on track.

## ⬟ CREATE A SAFE, CARING NEIGHBORHOOD

**Talk with your neighbors** to get everyone on board about not letting teens have parties unless a responsible adult is home. Ask them to let you know if they see unsafe activity going on when you're not home.

## ♥ PROVIDE FAMILY SUPPORT

**When teens feel good about themselves, they are less likely to turn to alcohol or other drugs to "feel better."** Look for ways to help your teen feel accepted and loved as he or she is. Spend time regularly with each of your teens. Try to have at least one meal together every day.

**If you think your teen has a substance abuse problem, don't try to cope alone or keep it a secret.** Changes in school performance or in how he or she usually behaves (e.g., missing curfew, abandoning old friends for a new crowd, lying, being unusually aggressive) may be warning signs.

You can get help from physicians, clergy, school counselors, librarians, caring teachers, relatives, and friends. An inpatient or outpatient drug treatment program may also be helpful. **Spend time with your teen doing things you both enjoy,** but don't feel you have to bring up "the problem" whenever you're together.

### MODEL RESTRAINT

Consider how *you* use alcohol or other drugs at home, informal get-togethers, parties, and elsewhere. **What messages are you sending to your teen**—is he or she learning that alcohol and other drugs are unappealing, frightening, enjoyable, helpful, or just for grown-ups?

### TEACH RESISTANCE SKILLS

**To help teens understand ways to resist pressure in social situations, emphasize that if they're clear about what they want, people will take them seriously.** Talk about your own experiences. Make sure your teen knows he or she can "use you as an excuse" to get out of difficult situation (e.g., "Forget it! My folks would never get off my back if they found out"). If it's comfortable, try role playing techniques to handle certain situations:

- ◆ Say no and give a reason ("No. Cigarette smoke makes my breath stink");
- ◆ Use humor ("Forget it. I'd rather go play on the freeway. It's safer");
- ◆ Apply pressure yourself ("No. I thought you were smarter than that"); or

◆ Always have an out ("Sorry, I can't stick around—promised my sister I'd take her to a movie")

## BE CREATIVE

Help your teen find creative outlets for his or her intense feelings rather than avoiding those feelings by using alcohol and other drugs. Expressing himself or herself through writing, painting, drawing, dancing, or other **artistic activities can be ways to turn difficult feelings into something life-affirming.**

## *FEEL ALIVE*

*Helping teens steer clear of substance use and abuse involves helping them feel strong enough to follow their own true path, even if the situation is a bit shaky. With the expectation that your daughter or son will succeed—and your continued acceptance when she or he doesn't—your teen is more likely to find her or his way.*

# Tragedy

*Your Dilemma:*

**"Our son's good friend died in a car accident last week. How do we help him find comfort?"**
*or*
**"Liza saw a tragic fire on TV, in which a girl her age died. Now she's afraid that something bad is going to happen to her, too."**

When a tragedy occurs close to home, whether it's a fatal accident, natural disaster, suicide, or shooting, we all struggle to make sense of life. Even a faraway terrorist attack can shift views of what is safe and will be okay. But teens especially may experience such intense reactions that they feel unable to talk about them, even with a parent. Helping your teen cope with the complicated feelings following a tragedy can be daunting, particularly if he or she withdraws in anger or sadness, acts as if nothing is wrong, or behaves recklessly. Yet, how you react to your teen's responses, as well as manage your own, can aid him or her in finding healthy ways to grieve and, ultimately, to carry on.

### ❤ COMMUNICATE POSITIVELY AS A FAMILY
**Avoid making any assumptions about what your teen knows, feels, or fears;** similarly, don't minimize pain or loss, disagree with her or him, or insist that your teen cheer up. Give your daughter or son your full attention when the two of you talk about what's going on, offer comfort, and assure her or him that the feelings are real and normal and that she or he will get through this. Simply being heard and acknowledged can be a great relief.

### ☺ PROMOTE CULTURAL COMPETENCE
Encourage your teen to not lash out against a particular group of people. **Reinforce that blaming a particular group** just because the people are part of the same religion, ethnicity, nationality, or socioeconomic class as those responsible for a particular tragedy **will only cause more harm.**

Using humor inappropriately—even without intending to be insensitive to others—may be one way your teen seeks to sort through feelings; try to help her or him understand that it's important to speak sincerely about underlying feelings.

### 🧭 BE HONEST
Your teen may want to talk about the same issues repeatedly. **When your daughter or son asks you questions, give honest answers. Try to remain calm and patient.** Your teen may also prefer to share her or his grief with friends—it can be comforting to know that friends feel similarly. Teens typ-

## Grappling with Tragedy

To help your teen grapple with the consequences of a tragedy and her or his place in the world, questions such as these may be useful:

◆ What is the worst part of the event?

◆ What sort of reactions did you have after experiencing or first hearing about the trauma? How about now?

◆ Are others at school or nearby struggling, too? Are some people's actions making things worse or better?

◆ Do you think you have a responsibility to help others in pain if you can? What if you don't even know them?

◆ What can we learn from what happened?

ically have many philosophical questions and a need to explore issues to understand whatever happened.

**Let your teen know what your own feelings are.** If you show that you have strong and sometimes confused feelings but can also take steps to heal, your example will help provide context for her or his own feelings.

### ENSURE SAFETY

Reassure your teen that you're doing all you can to keep your family safe. Some helpful words may include "the event is over," "together we can help get things back to normal," or "we can become safer and stronger as a result of what's happened." Emphasize other personal or national tragedies in the past that have happened (e.g., school shootings, September 11th) and how people do survive crises. **Talk specifically about how you're encouraged by all that others have done to help.**

To help work through the pain, **remind your teen that it's important to connect with others**—extended family, caring adults in the neighborhood or at your school, congregation, or community club, supportive peers. One of the biggest dangers in the midst of tragedy is individuals and families becoming more isolated and depending on themselves only.

### ✪ SERVE OTHERS
**Turning troubled feelings into positive action by helping others often provides relief** from the helplessness that accompanies loss. Encourage your teen to:

- ◆ Start a neighborhood drive to raise money for victims or for a memorial fund;
- ◆ Create cards, write letters, or bake cookies for the families of victims;
- ◆ Participate in a memorial service or create a monument for the victims;
- ◆ Offer practical help, such as grocery shopping, to families if appropriate;
- ◆ Volunteer at an established relief organization, such as the Red Cross; or
- ◆ Join a political action group to address causes.

## *SEE A BRIGHTER FUTURE*

*When tragedy strikes, the veneer of self-sufficiency that teens work so hard to display can be quickly stripped away. By demonstrating your own vulnerability and resilience, you can help your teen rebuild faith in the future and the world.*

# 40 Developmental Assets for Adolescents
## (Ages 12–18)

Search Institute has identified the following building blocks of healthy development that help young people grow up healthy, caring, and responsible.

## EXTERNAL ASSETS
### Support
1. **Family support**—Family life provides high levels of love and support.
2. **Positive family communication**—Young person and her or his parent(s) communicate positively, and young person is willing to seek advice and counsel from parents.
3. **Other adult relationships**—Young person receives support from three or more nonparent adults.
4. **Caring neighborhood**—Young person experiences caring neighbors.
5. **Caring school climate**—School provides a caring, encouraging environment.
6. **Parent involvement in schooling**—Parent(s) are actively involved in helping young person succeed in school.

### Empowerment
7. **Community values youth**—Young person perceives that adults in the community value youth.
8. **Youth as resources**—Young people are given useful roles in the community.
9. **Service to others**—Young person serves in the community one hour or more per week.
10. **Safety**—Young person feels safe at home, at school, and in the neighborhood.

### Boundaries and Expectations
11. **Family boundaries**—Family has clear rules and consequences and monitors the young person's whereabouts.
12. **School boundaries**—School provides clear rules and consequences.

13. **Neighborhood boundaries**—Neighbors take responsibility for monitoring young people's behavior.
14. **Adult role models**—Parent(s) and other adults model positive, responsible behavior.
15. **Positive peer influence**—Young person's best friends model responsible behavior.
16. **High expectations**—Both parent(s) and teachers encourage the young person to do well.

### Constructive Use of Time
17. **Creative activities**—Young person spends three or more hours per week in lessons or practice in music, theater, or other arts.
18. **Youth programs**—Young person spends three or more hours per week in sports, clubs, or organizations at school and/or in the community.
19. **Religious community**—Young person spends one or more hours per week in activities in a religious institution.
20. **Time at home**—Young person is out with friends "with nothing special to do" two or fewer nights per week.

## INTERNAL ASSETS
### Commitment to Learning
21. **Achievement motivation**—Young person is motivated to do well in school.
22. **School engagement**—Young person is actively engaged in learning.
23. **Homework**—Young person reports doing at least one hour of homework every school day.
24. **Bonding to school**—Young person cares about her or his school.
25. **Reading for pleasure**—Young person reads for pleasure three or more hours per week.

### Positive Values
26. **Caring**—Young person places high value on helping other people.
27. **Equality and social justice**—Young person places high value on promoting equality and reducing hunger and poverty.
28. **Integrity**—Young person acts on convictions and stands up for her or his beliefs.
29. **Honesty**—Young person "tells the truth even when it is not easy."

30. **Responsibility**—Young person accepts and takes personal responsibility.
31. **Restraint**—Young person believes it is important not to be sexually active or to use alcohol or other drugs.

## Social Competencies
32. **Planning and decision making**—Young person knows how to plan ahead and make choices.
33. **Interpersonal competence**—Young person has empathy, sensitivity, and friendship skills.
34. **Cultural competence**—Young person has knowledge of and comfort with people of different cultural/racial/ethnic backgrounds.
35. **Resistance skills**—Young person can resist negative peer pressure and dangerous situations.
36. **Peaceful conflict resolution**—Young person seeks to resolve conflict nonviolently.

## Positive Identity
37. **Personal power**—Young person feels he or she has control over "things that happen to me."
38. **Self-esteem**—Young person reports having a high self-esteem.
39. **Sense of purpose**—Young person reports that "my life has a purpose."
40. **Positive view of personal future**—Young person is optimistic about her or his personal future.

# Parent's Developmental Assets
# **Daily Checklist**

Use the developmental assets to help you choose the ways you want to intentionally build the strengths of your teen. Try using this checklist or create your own.

## *Today I will:*

- ❏ Ask how my teen is doing. (Asset 2)

- ❏ Really listen to my teen. (Asset 33)

- ❏ Act responsibly (Asset 30)

- ❏ Be honest with my spouse (partner), kids, friends, neighbors— even salespeople. (Asset 29)

- ❏ Offer my teen opportunities to contribute to the family and to other people. (Assets 7, 8, 9)

- ❏ Notice what's happening in my neighborhood. (Asset 13)

- ❏ Ask what my teen learned, liked, and didn't like in school. (Asset 6)

- ❏ Tell my teen about my day. (Asset 2)

- ❏ Keep track of what my teen is doing. (Asset 11)

- ❏ Provide a quiet place for homework. (Asset 23)

- ❏ Know when to turn off the TV. (Asset 20)

- ❏ Give my teen ways to grow in body, mind, and spirit. (Assets 17, 18, 19)

- ❏ Tell my teen one thing I love or appreciate about her or him. (Asset 38)

# Helpful Resources for Parents and Teens

To learn more about the developmental assets and how to use them, take a look at these resources available from Search Institute through our Web site at www.search-institute.org. Check out our online catalog for even more videos, books, posters, and workbooks too.

## FOR PARENTS

*"Ask Me Where I'm Going" and Other Revealing Messages from Today's Teens.* What teens want to tell the adults in their lives, they tell you here in this gift book in their own evocative words. Their inspirational statements and requests will help you think about ways you can connect with teens to give them what they want—the same things that research shows they need for success. A must-read for all adults—not just parents and teachers.

*Connect 5: Finding the Caring Adults You May Not Realize Your Teen Needs* by Kathleen Kimball-Baker. Plenty of compelling evidence shows that it is through relationships with caring adults—parents and nonparents—that young people build many of the skills, strengths, and the resilience they need to grow up happy and productive; but unfortunately many barriers keep adults and teens from connecting in meaningful ways. Speaking directly to parents, this motivating book helps parents identify the kinds of responsible, caring adults who can teach their teens new skills, listen without judgment, lighten the mood, and support the values parents work so hard to instill. Inspiring tips, ideas, and stories help parents understand how to reach out to such adults.

*Tag, You're It! 50 Easy Ways to Connect with Young People* by Kathleen Kimball-Baker. Written in an easy-to-read format, this inspiring book offers commonsense ideas for connecting and building assets with young people. Youth workers, parents, educators, businesspeople, congregation leaders, and anyone who cares about youth will love this book. Use the *Tag, You're It!* card deck to spark conversations between youth and adults and raise awareness about asset building.

*Taking Asset Building Personally.* With the planning and discussion guide plus six copies of the action and reflection workbook, you'll have everything you need to work in a small parents' group or book club. Fun, thought-provoking, and filled with ideas and information.

*The Asset Approach* (Spanish version available). Informative and concise, this 8-page handout introduces adults to the power of using the 40 developmental assets in daily interactions with young people.

## FOR TEENS

*An Asset Builder's Guide to Youth and Money* by Jolene L. Roehlkepartain. This practical guide takes a positive approach to empowering young people to build competency in financial areas such as earning, spending, investing, saving, and giving.

*Step by Step! A Young Person's Guide to Positive Community Change* by the Mosaic Youth Center Board members and Jennifer Griffin-Wiesner. To quote the young people who cowrote this guide, "You don't have to be famous or brilliant or rich to make a difference. You just have to care and then do something about it." They provide the ideas and tools for other young people to make change in their community—including how to involve adults to help—and share the tips and trials of their own work to get a new community center built in their neighborhood.

*Succeed Every Day: Daily Readings for Teens* by Pamela Espeland. Published by Free Spirit Publishing. Each day's passage is formatted with a famous quote, a brief bit of related wisdom, and an affirmation to carry teens positively through the day.